WARNING

* WARNING *

If you hate the word Bum
I think you'd better run
If you don't like to fart,
and you think you're too smart
to read this silly nonsense,
with its very silly contents,
Then you'd better take up knitting,
or go and do some fishing

BUT

You'd better beware,
If you read it, if you dare,
It will be lots of fun,
and you'll learn, a big fat ton,
about the stuff of life,
You might wanna read it twice,
There's lots of info too,
On things that may be new,
So come on, have a geezer,
Don't worry about your Mom,
In the end, this book will please her!!

OTHER BOOKS BY KATE CULLEN

Dedication

This is for all the kids who love their computer games, but like to read as well. It's also for the parents who want their kids to read, but can't find anything they like. And a big thankyou to teachers for inspiring kids to read and helping them in their journey to discovering the big wide world out there through reading.

Game on Boys 3

NO GIRLS ALLOWED!

Written and Illustrated by Kate Cullen
Copyright © 2015 @ Kate Cullen

CONTENTS

1. The Good News and the Bad News

Two really super-duper awesome things happened to me the other week, all on the one day. I just have to tell you about them before I bust my guts. You are not going to believe it. And before you go getting too excited for me, no, I didn't get the latest PlayStation 5 or the new Nintendo DS 3. Wish I had, but I know that's not going to happen in a hurry; not with my stingy parents anyway. "Money doesn't grow on trees you know," they say. Yeah I know, but if I ever forget, I know my parents will remind me like, another five hundred and fifty-six times before I die. They should make a recording. It would last longer.

Unfortunately, on exactly the same day, my wild excitement was totally hacked by another event that was absolutely, insanely mortifying. It was the most shocking, most horrific disaster you can ever imagine; so big, I can't even bear thinking about it. Do you get the picture? It was like **BAD.**

When it happened, it was like the world was over. School was never going to be the same again. I was so shocked that I didn't even *want* to go to school. But my mom forced me, by pushing me out the door. She's a girl so she would never understand the humiliation of it all.

Where do I even start? Do you want the bad news or the good news? That's what my dad always says when he's got bad news, but there's *never* any good news. He usually says, "the bad news is, there's no good news, and the really bad news is…blah blah."

In case you've forgotten, my name is Ryan. Some of my friends call me Rino. Some of my enemies do too, but I haven't got many enemies, just Lisa, my sister. She calls me other names too, but not to my face. Actually, no, that's wrong. She does call them to my face. But sometimes she likes me, and sometimes I like her, like once a year, at Christmas time when she gives me an awesome present, usually bought by Mom.

I don't know if you remember how insanely awesome my school is. Yeah, no school is awesome, like **everrrrrrrrrrrrr.** But seriously, my school is. Well it used to be anyway, until last term, when a mad, running obsessed teacher replaced our regular teacher, Mr Higginbottom. He used to let us play PlayStation at school. No–one ever believed me when I told them that. But he makes us work hard for it. We work our butts off actually. Maybe that's why his surname is Higginbottom, because he makes us work our 'butts' off. Get it? Bottom! Butts.

He even organized this big PlayStation competition at the start of the year for the boys and had PS games as the prize, and guess who won. The best ever gamer in the fifth grade won, that's who. **ME!!**

Life was so cool at school, until the dreaded Dorkster took over, because Mr Higginbottom had to go and look after his sick Mother. The Dorkster was a grumpy teacher called Miss Dorklands, who was obsessed with running. Instead of having our normal PlayStation club, we got to have a running club. Yey, Yey, Double Yey. **NOT!** She thought we all did so well in the daily running that she turned it into an afterschool voluntary club thing too. I think she got about three kids to join. Of course my goody goody mate Josh was the first to sign up. I said I had band practice that night, even though I'm not a member of any band. I don't even play an instrument.

Mr Higginbottom was only supposed to be gone for four weeks. That was like a life sentence in prison when you knew you had to do algebra, spelling, and history, followed by running EVERYDAY.

On the first day of the fifth week, I rocked up to school with this mammoth smile plastered across my face because I expected Mr Higginbottom to be waiting at his desk.

I even bought him a chocolate bar to welcome him back. Well I can tell you, that smile got wiped off my face pretty quickly when I rocked into class and saw Miss Dorklands happily writing up algebra sums on the blackboard, AGAIN! I mean seriously, who does algebra in the fifth grade? Isn't that something reserved for senior school?

So we had to suffer along with Miss Dorklands and her little running fixation for the rest of the school term. But that's not even the bad news. It gets worse.

2. The Good, the Bad and the Ugly

I remember the day really clearly. It's like one of those days stamped so firmly on your brain, that even when you're an old grandpa sitting on your rocking chair telling tales to your grandkids, you can still remember it, like it was yesterday.

My Pop always used to do that. He'd sit talking to us saying, "I remember the day when there were no computers, no iPhones, and not even any TV's." WOW! I am so glad I didn't live in Pop's era. They were so deprived. He probably got to see living dinosaurs roaming around though.

I'd woken up really early that day, to take the dogs for a walk. We were babysitting (dog-sitting) two dogs that belonged to an old man who was in hospital. It was awesome having pets to talk to again. The only pet I have, is a dirty, big rat in the roof that keeps talking to me when I'm trying to get to sleep, so it's like a dream come true having Tess and Maxi to look after.

When the rest of the family are being annoying, I can just go out and chill with the dogs. I can tell them my problems, and they listen to me without giving any cheek back. The only thing they give me is big slobbery kisses planted on my face.

I knew that they would probably be going back to Bob, their owner soon, so I wanted to make sure I walked them every day. Mom always reminds me that it's all very well to have fun with dogs, but you have to look after their needs as well, and that means feeding them, walking them, brushing them, and unfortunately PICKING UP THEIR POOP! But I know she's right, so I do it without complaining.

On this particular day, I got up and was putting on their leads, giving them extra big cuddles because I was starting to feel really sad about them leaving. Mom had said the day before, "all good things must come to an end." Yeah right, don't I know it. She tells me that every time it's time to turn Minecraft off.

Dad walked in before he left for work. "Morning son."

"Hi Dad."

"Do you want the bad news or the good news?" he said. Here we go, I thought. He'll say, "the bad news is, there's no good news, and the really bad news is........." I waited for it. What was it going to be this time? My heart started thudding just waiting to hear Dad's really bad news.

3. Poor Little Princess, Pain in the Butt

Lisa walked in, just as Dad was about to tell me the bad news. She was all in a panic because she couldn't find her homework.

"You could say the dog ate it," I volunteered, laughing at her.

"Der! As if my teacher would believe that. And anyway, I already used that excuse last week when I forgot to do it."

"Lisa. Where were you doing it last night?" Dad began.

"Ahhh. I can't remember. Did I do any last night? No, the last time I did it was in Mom's car on Friday. Oh NO! It's in Mom's car. DAD! You have to go and pick it up. Or I'll get in trouble by Mr Grumpy."

"Excuse me princess, I don't *have* to do anything. Especially when you order me about in a tone like that. And don't call Mr

Grund, Mr Grumpy." About time Dad said something about Lisa's bossy attitude. She does think she's a princess and the rest of us are her slaves in waiting.

"Dad!" I interrupted. "You were going to tell me the news."

"What? Oh that. Look, that can wait. We need to sort something out about getting Lisa's homework, otherwise she'll get in trouble by Mr Grumpy." He winked at me.

"Can't you just write her a note?"

"A note? Saying what? *Please don't let my poor little princess get in trouble.*" Dad laughed at himself.

"No, just make up some excuse that she hasn't got it. Mom does it all the time." She never does. Mom wouldn't dare make up excuses for us, but Dad didn't have to know that minor detail.

"No Dad. Please can't you just go to Mom's work on the way?" Lisa harped on. *Poor little princess, pain in the butt* I thought to myself.

"Well I think I like Rino's idea better. It's quicker," Dad decided.

"But Da.."

"Ah. No buts Lisa. I don't like butts and I don't have time to be gallivanting all over the country side. Now get me some note paper please."

"Dad! What's the news?" I tried to get him focused on what he started to tell me again .

"Later son, we'll talk about it when you get home from school. The missing homework will have to take priority here." Ruined again by Lisa. She had a habit of ruining things. It was God's gift to her.

It was probably going to be bad news anyway. What would happen if Dad said he got a promotion and we were moving towns? I might never see Mr Higginbottom and his PlayStations again.

I worried about the news all the way to school. Was it really going to be good or was it going to be one of Dad's disastrously embarrassing fiascos? Who would know with my Dad.

But by the time I got to the school and entered the gates, Dad's good or bad news had gone right out the window, because the best ever news was waiting right inside the class room for me. All my Christmases had come at once. In fact it was like all the Christmases, birthdays, Easter eggs, and holidays had all come together. It was AWESOME!

4. The Best News like Everrrrrrrrrrr!

The first person I saw was Miss Dorklands, our substitute teacher, with her coffee cup doing yard duty. "Good Morning Ryan," she said pleasantly.

"Morning Miss," I replied. Despite the fact that she made us run all the time and we didn't get to have the PS club, I had actually come to like Miss Dorklands. She was the one who taught me to have courage and determination in an experience that saved my life earlier in the year. Never before had I come so close to death in the most frightening event of my life. But to my surprise, at the time, it was her words ringing in my ears that made me hang on. So I guess she's ok.

"I've changed the night of the running club Rino, so you could probably join us now," she offered.

"Ahh, I have to…ah, I have to……. practice my trombone that night," I stuttered quickly.

"But I didn't tell you what night it was on."

"Well I have to practice it every night, that's why I can't do other stuff, like never, never- ever, ever, everrrrr."

"Shame. You show such promise in running." The only promise I was going to make, was a promise to myself that I wouldn't do running out of choice. Forced into it, yep, I would do it, but I wasn't going to make a conscious decision to do extra body bashing of my own free will. That would be like, psycho!

"I didn't know you played two instruments."

"I don't, just the trombone," I answered, puzzled.

"Oh, I thought the other day you said you played the trumpet."

"Oh. Did I? That's because I meant to say trombone. Because I really want to play the trumpet. I got confused. But it's the trumpet I really play. Ah… I mean the trombone. I really play the trombone." I was getting myself in deeper and deeper with every lie. I hated lying, but not as much as I hated running.

"Trombone? Who plays the trombone?" My friend Matthew had just appeared out of nowhere, ready to give the game away if I didn't get out of there quick.

"Ok, see you in class Miss Dorki, ahh Dorklands." I nearly let her nick name slip, as I grabbed Matthew by the arm and dragged him off towards our class room.

"Actually….." Miss Dorklands started to say something but I pretended I didn't hear as I dragged Matthew away.

"You nearly got me busted!" I exclaimed.

"What? What did I do?"

"Miss Dorki thinks I play the trombone."

"Why would she think a dumb thing like that?"

"She just does."

"And why does she?"

"Do we have to play the twenty question game?"

"Yep!"

"Because I told her I was in the band to get out of the running club."

"Bahahaha. WHAT? You're the most unmusical kid I know, except for myself."

"Aw funny haha. Well it worked, didn't it?" I replied smugly.

"What a whoppa. Just for that, I'm going to give you a whoppa." As soon as he said the words, I knew what was coming next, but before I had a chance to run, Matthew had let the biggest fart explode in my direction. Matthew never missed an opportunity to let one rip.

PPPFFFFFFFTT !!!

"Phewie you stink bomb," I glared at him, even though it was a pretty regular occurrence to have to face his blasters.

"Hey, do you want the good news or the bad news?" Matthew changed the subject, suddenly gleaming with excitement.

"Aw man, what is it about the good news and the bad news today? Every man and his dog has good news and bad news. What news?" I said impatiently.

"Settle petal. Do you want me to tell you or not?"

"Only if it's good news," I answered. "If it's bad news, you can squish on it with one of your stinky, squelchy liquid farts for all I care." Just as Matthew was about to open his mouth, our other friend Josh came bounding up to us in a frenzy. He was gleaming from ear to ear.

"Oh my god! Oh my god! I can't believe it," he said. "Have you heard the news?"

"Is it good news or bad news?" I asked. It was getting really boring, all these people dangling 'news' in front of me but not actually spilling the beans as to what the news really was.

"If you're thinking what I'm thinking," Matthew started, "then YES. I saw the news with my own two eyes. It's so exciting, it deserves a happy fart," and again, right on cue, Matthew let one rip.

BRRRRFLT!!!

"Matthew!!" Josh and I both exploded simultaneously.

"Would someone please tell me the news before I do a big fart on your head Matthew?" I pleaded.

"EW! Gross!" Matthew replied. He screwed his face up like a one year old mushroom festering at the bottom of the fridge.

"No, let him see for himself," Josh suggested.

"Yeah, ok, cool," Matthew agreed.

"Oh come on guys. What the hek is it?"

"Follow us," and they raced off towards our classroom before I could complain. Josh was sprinting so fast, I had no chance of catching up to him once he had a head start on me.

"WAIT UP," I called out, but they had gone faster than a speeding bullet. I really didn't think there was going to be any exciting news, but I followed them anyway. But when I got to the final destination, I realized how wrong I was. The news was AWESOME!

Awesome

5. How to Train a Bully

As they rounded the corner, I watched in horror as they sprinted past a kid called Nigel standing next to a locker. Josh was too fast for Nigel, but as Mattie ran past, Nigel stuck his foot out and nastily tripped him up. That's why we call him Nasty Nige. He can't help himself doing nasty things all the time.

There was an unfamiliar girl standing next to him and I think I saw a little snigger escape from the corner of her mouth as she watched Mattie fall. Nigel was probably showing off to her.

"NIGEL!" Matthew yelled, as he lurched forward.

"NIGEL!" I yelled.

"NIGEL," Josh echoed, as he turned to see what was going on, just as Matthew did an awesome nose plant into the gravel.

"You…you…." Matthew was holding in his anger as he lay on the ground shaking his fist at Nigel. Even though we know bullying sucks, we know it's useless fighting back and joining the violence.

As tempting as it was to go and bop Nigel on the nose, I resisted, knowing that it would only cause more trouble. Plus, he also had a really slimy boogie hanging out of his nostril and I didn't particularly want to contaminate my fist with his green goober.

I could see Matthew starting to get agro on the ground, so I butted in. "Cool it, dude," I said to my mate. "What's up your beef?" I directed at Nigel. "Why did you have to go and do a lousy thing like that?"

"Felt like it," Nigel said smugly. "Nuff'n else to do." He looked around at the girl who was by his side. He was definitely showing off to her. She might have even put him up to it. I didn't know who she was, but she looked a bit mean.

"Seriously!" Matthew exclaimed, as he got up and dusted the gravel off his knees. "Where did you get your brains? Out of a cereal packet?"

"Matthew!" I said, under my breath. "He's not worth it." Matthew could get a bit feisty at times when he was provoked, and I really didn't feel like breaking up any fights before school.

"Remember what I told you about the size of his sausage dog? That's why he has to make up for it, by being a bully, so just feel sorry for him and let it go."

"What sausage dog? I don't care if he has a dog or a cat or a canary with a wooden leg. It doesn't give him the right just to trip people up."

"No! You know what I heard the psychologist say on that movie," I whispered, "that boys with small wieners try and make up for it by bullying, to try and assert their power." Matthew chuckled.

"Oh yeah, alright." He turned his attention to Nigel, and spoke in a very sarcastically pleasant voice. "Nigel, please do not act like that. It makes you look dumb, and it makes me feel bad, not to mention quite sore on my knees, where the blood is gushing forth like sauce does from a meat pie."

All the teachers and parents always say, instead of fighting back, always let the bully know how you feel and politely ask them to stop the offending behavior. Yeah right! Nigel just laughed in his face. But we kept walking. Matthew was limping a bit, but I think he was faking it for some sympathy.

"Aw he's so nasty," Josh said, as we walked away.

"Yeah, he's nasty boy Nige. And he's bad. Bad, Bad, BAD!"

BAD BAD BAD

"Yeah, he's so bad, he probably goes to have a whiz, and doesn't even wash his hands," I added.

"What's so bad about that?" Matthew looked at me puzzled.

"Eewgh," I answered.

"And he's so bad, he probably picks his nose and doesn't wash his hands," Josh added.

"And he's so bad," Matthew continued chuckling, "he probably picks his nose, eats it and doesn't wash his hands." We all started laughing hysterically.

Then I added, really getting carried away, " he's so bad, he probably picks his nose, eats it, licks his fingers, then dips his fingers in the chocolate spread and puts it back in the cupboard."

"Oh gross out. Now I feel sick," Josh said, doubling over in peals of laughter. At least we had helped Matthew forget about his anger towards Nigel. But in doing so, I had forgotten that we were running towards the good news, so when I got to our classroom and saw it, I was so excited, I nearly started squealing like a girl. But I had to do my squeals inside, as it definitely wouldn't have looked too cool. So deep down in the pit of my stomach where the gooey bits have a party, I screamed,

"Squeeeeeeeeeeeeeeeeeeeeeeeeeeeee," like a big dumb girl.

6. Double Awesomeness

The awesome news.

There it was, or should I say, there 'he' was. As we approached our classroom, Matthew self-importantly said to me, as though he was presenting me with a real life royal castle from a Minecraft city, "have a gander inside the window."

"What? It's just our classroom? What could be so exciting in a classroom?" I enquired, before an exciting thought suddenly caused my heart to skip a beat, and my breath to quicken.

"JUST LOOK WILL YOU!" ordered Josh, and I shut my eyes quickly to do a quick prayer in a nano second (a micro nano prayer), and opened them to see *the* most famous, *the* most awesome, *the* best teacher to ever roam this earth. He was writing maths sums onto the board and I was screaming so hard inside, my guts were about to burst.

"AWESOME!" I shouted.

"Double awesome," Matthew agreed. "Do you think he will start up the PS club again?"

"Yeah of course dummy," Josh replied. "As if he wouldn't."

"Probably," I added, though I was more excited at the thought of Mr Higginbottom returning than the PlayStation club. Ever since my family started babysitting the dogs, I haven't been as obsessed as playing computer games as I used to be. I mean, I don't think I was ever obsessed with them, but my Mom had this crazy notion in her head that I was.

I heard her saying to her friend the other day that I had lost my obsession since we got the dogs. What would she know? She has no idea how educational and informative computer games can be, and how they can stimulate creative thoughts, and challenge our minds to think strategically. Not to mention all the exercise our wrists, hands and arms get. I must remember to remind Mom of those facts next time she complains about me being on the Xbox too long.

"Shall we go in and see him?" I suggested. I really wanted to say hello before all the girls took up his attention.

"Nah. Let's just leave him be, until the bell goes. Come on, let's go play handball in the undercover area," Matthew said.

Mr Higginbottom's homecoming was as exciting for me as it was for everybody. Apart from the fact that he allowed some of the boys to play PlayStation *at school* every Friday afternoon if they worked hard, he was just an awesome teacher. He was very funny and very caring, and he made learning fun. Even the girls who didn't care about computer games (thank goodness) loved him. He was definitely the best teacher ever.

On the first day of school this year, he wrote his name on the blackboard and made us all shout out "BOTTOM BOTTOM BOTTOM," just to get the silliness out of our system. But this time when we all walked into class to see him returned, he shouted in one of his crazy accents, "Yes folks, the great big *butt* is back, direct from *Uranus,* straight from the *bottom* of the state, and landing *behind* the desk in order to work your butts off, by teaching you the wonders of the ABC and the marvels of mathematics."

I had no idea what he was going on about, but he was using such a silly voice I couldn't help joining in with everyone laughing hysterically.

"So, shake your tail feathers kids and get your rear end into gear, because we have a lot of awesome learning to do, and a lot of awesome......you guessed it kiddie widdies, an awesome lot of *gaming* to do. That's right folks, you heard it first from the biggest bottom this side of the moon. Let the gaming begin." There were masses of cheers from the boys, and a lot of disgruntled murmurs from the girls. Girls were not allowed in the PlayStation club. It was a rule. Actually, it wasn't a formal rule, but no girl ever wanted to get in the club, so we didn't have to worry about it.

28

Matthew and I looked at each other with gleaming eyes. Matthew's eyes were bulging so far, they looked like they were about to pop out of their socket. Josh also had this really happy look on his face like he'd just seen Santa Claus coming down the chimney. In fact all the boys were looking extremely cheerful. If we took a selfie of all our faces, no-one would believe we were at school on a Monday morning about to start work.

"So, let's get this awesome day started by getting the butt jokes out of the way. Who's got a new one for me? A new butt joke. Anyone, anyone?"

Peter had his hand waving madly in the air.

"Yes Peter. It better not be one of your old ones Peter."

"Why did the toilet paper roll down the hill?"

"No idea Peter. Maybe because it did a rolling hill start? No idea."

Someone yelled from the back of the class, "because it wanted to get to the bottom." The class roared with laughter. It was an old joke, but it was funny saying it in class in front of a teacher.

My dad once said to me, "I hope your life is like a toilet paper roll." I was offended until he said, "may it be *long* and *useful*." I thought about telling that one to Mr H, but I didn't think most of the kids would get it, and Jacob had put up his hand.

"I have one Mr H."

"Ok last one, Jacob."

"What happened when the toilet paper rolled down the hill?"

No-one answered, so he answered his own riddle with a big, cheesy grin on his face. "It got stuck in the crack." Again, the class roared.

"And da da da da da dat's all folks," Mr H said, like he was Porky Pig. "We got to the bottom of our lungs with our laughter, now it's time for the serious stuff. But before we start Maths, I would like to introduce you to our new student, who is the luckiest student in the world to arrive on my first day back into the best fifth grade class in the world."

Every-one started looking around the mat to see who the new student was. It would be awesome to have another boy to compete in the PlayStation club. As my thoughts started thinking about the new opposition in the club, Mr H said, "please stand up and introduce yourself to the class."

As the new student stood up sheepishly, waves of horror swept over me. I was as horrified as an ant looking up towards an elephant's foot descending upon his head.

7. The Baddest, Worstest News, like Everrrrrrrrrrrrr

I was horrified when I saw the new student slowly stand up, for three reasons, and in no particular order, because they were all bad. Bad, Bad, Bad!

1. Because the new student was a girl.

2. It was the same girl who was standing next to Nigel when he tripped up Matthew. The same girl who sniggered when it happened.

3. I didn't know about number 3, but it was coming.

The new girl stood up from behind Nigel. It was no wonder I hadn't noticed her, Nigel's big boof head was in the way. I wondered if she was going to be as mean as Nigel was, and whether she had put him up to the tripping incident.

"Tell us about yourself," Mr Higginbottom prompted.

"Ahh, my name is Elly. I have just moved to this area for my Dad's job. I have one sister who is only four, and ahh…she's a brat." The class laughed at this, which made smelly Elly a little more relaxed. Initially she had been standing as stiff as a post, like she'd been superglued together.

"What are your favorite hobbies Elly?" I waited for her to say dancing, ice skating, Instagram and facetiming, like all the other girls, but she surprised me with her answer.

"I like computer games heaps. Minecraft is my favorite. I play it on my Xbox, and I also like to go cross country running, and I'd like to be in the school band." Eeewwgh, running *and* the band. BORING. But computer games? Everyone was a bit shocked when she said she liked computer games, especially the boys. Not a lot of girls would admit to that. Maybe she was a tom boy, which would explain why she egged Nigel on to trip up Matthew.

This girl was going to be trouble. I could see it already, especially if she was going to hang around Nigel. Double trouble! She looked a bit rough, not neatly dressed like the other girls. She was wearing khaki shorts with a baggy t-shirt with 'Zombies rule' emblazoned across the front. There was not one bit of pink to be seen, not even in her hair which was an unruly mess of brown curls.

I looked over to Josh so I could screw up my nose, signalling my dislike for the new tom boy in the class, but to my horror, Josh was looking up at her with his eyes hanging out of his head, and he had this really goofy look on his face. I felt like yelling at him to put

his tongue back into his mouth. She wasn't even pretty. Maybe he just went all goo gaa at the sound of the word Minecraft.

"Well thankyou Elly," Mr Higginbottom said. "I hope you enjoy this school. I'm sure you'll find it a very friendly and welcoming place. Sophie, would you mind being Elly's buddy and helping her out today if she needs it?"

"Yes Sir Mr Higginbottom," Sophie beamed. She loved to suck up to the teachers, so it would be a real treat for Sophie to help.

"Now class, before we get on with the important part of the day, I'd like to tempt you with a teaser. If you work well, before lunch, I will announce what's going to be happening with the PS Club now that I'm back. There are some changes that will be happening and also something you might find just a little bit exciting. Anyone interested in hearing the news should stay for five minutes into the lunch break." I looked around listening to the girls moaning and whinging, but the boys were all gleaming excitedly.

Nigel looked over at me smugly and whispered, "You're going down this time Rino. I'm going to smash you!" I laughed at his hopeful dreaming, but as I looked past Nigel, towards the new girl, my laughter soured as I saw her looking excited at the news.

Seriously! I have never seen a girl look excited at any PS Club news. She couldn't….she wouldn't want to………NOOOOO! She must have been smiling at something else. There is no way a girl would even think about joining the club. No girls are allowed anyway. That's the rules!

As the morning went on, Matthew, Josh and I couldn't stop talking about the fact that Mr H was back and he was going to make an announcement about the PS club already. Luckily he was in a really good mood and we didn't have to do much Maths or English. We got to go outside and play a game of mini soccer, followed by Red Rover.

After playing outside, we came in and played the cool game 'Space Jump' where you have to improvise and speak really quickly or you're out. It's really funny because everyone always gets tongue tied and says weird things as they try to speak rapidly.

I got kicked out by Grace because she never stops talking, so she's had plenty of practice. I got stumped and Peter took my place. It was hilarious as they ended up talking about names and things in the garden for some strange reason. The conversation went something like this,

"Hi,"

"Hi." Then they both giggled, embarrassed by their nervousness.

"What's your name?" Peter continued quickly.

"My name's April."

"So……. you're a month?"

"Well yes actually, and I'm also a season. My middle name is Summer."

"So I suppose you're a day of the week too."

"Yes that's right. My surname is Sunday."

"So your name is April Summer Sunday?" Peter said, looking chuffed with himself as the class began to chuckle.

"Yup!"

"That's a weird name," Peter continued.

"Well what's your name?

"Peter Oliver Olden," he said, giving his real name.

"So your initials are P.O.O? I think that's weirder," Grace replied, and the class burst out laughing, but Peter blushed and was lost for words. The rule is that you can't pause for more than three seconds so he started fumbling for something to say. Then it was like a light bulb went on in his brain, as his face lit up brightly.

"So my initials might be weird, but your initials spell ASS. That's worse."

I have never heard the class laugh so loudly. It was like a congregation of giggling hyenas were having their annual meeting. Everyone was shrieking and wriggling uncontrollably all over the place.

Then someone yelled out from the back, "that means you two go together, ass and poo," and once again, the class lost all control of their laughing gear.

Amongst the noise and uncontrolled commotion, a loud squelchy blast made itself known. I looked around at Matthew who was sitting behind me. He was still laughing, but he managed to squeak out between tears, "it was an accident. I couldn't help it. I can't control that end when I'm laughing so hard at the other end." And he doubled over hysterically, but Mr H started to get his serious face on as the class screamed wildly.

"Ok class, we're getting out of control here. The jokes are getting a bit gross. Let's keep it clean. Matthew take a walk outside and air yourself please, and Peter and Grace, get on with it or I'll pick two other people. And keep the conversation away from posterior matters." Mr H's face showed he was serious, so we all settled down quickly.

"Ok, so ah……." Peter began, trying to stifle his laughter. "What did you do on the weekend?"

"I helped my dad plant some barsely, I mean basil and parsley." Grace laughed at herself.

"Was it fun?" Peter fired back rapidly.

"Yes I like planting arsely."

As the words arsely came out of Grace's mouth, the whole class erupted into peals of laughter yet again. It sounded so hilarious because they were speaking so fast and it just blurted out. Grace kept doubling over with her face all squashed up laughing, but no sound was coming out. Even Mr H bellowed out loud, even though he was trying with great difficulty to keep a straight face .

Grace continued with her kitchen talk. "We also mixed some oranges, apples and parsley in a salad for dinner."

"Gross," Peter said. "What do you call that?"

"An orange arsley salad," Grace said, as she squealed at her own ridiculous words.

After that last comment, Mr Higginbottom wrapped it up and declared there was no winner because everyone was too obsessed with talking about bottoms.

As lunch time approached, all the boys began to get excited because it had been so long since we'd had the PlayStation club at school, and we couldn't wait to hear what was going to happen with it.

When the bell rang, Mr Higginbottom told us all to go to lunch. Josh looked over at me puzzled. I looked at Matthew, who in turn looked at Jacob. We all had these dopey looking expressions on our faces wondering whether he'd forgotten about the announcement. No-one was saying anything until finally Josh piped up and asked the question we were all thinking.

"Mr Higginbottom, weren't you going to make an announcement about the PS Club?"

He glanced up with a confused look on his face. His eyebrows were poking down reaching for his nose in a puzzled manner. "What PS Club?" he said. "I thought that was finished, replaced with the awesome running club."

I was stunned. I didn't believe the words I was hearing. Had Mr H had some sort of memory brain fart? What was going on? I have a little green gremlin that lives in my veins, and surfs around my blood stream, hanging ten.

When things go wrong, it gets angry and starts attacking the walls of my veins, pounding to get out, and I could feel it happening big time as I panicked that the running club was going to take over the PS Club. *THIS CAN NOT HAPPEN,* I thought to myself. NEVER! NEVER! NEVER!

8. GOTCHA!

All the other boys were lingering around sharing dumbfounded expressions, not knowing what to say as Mr Higginbottom kept shuffling papers on his desk. It was like he was ignoring us. The girls filtered out slowly, but not before leaving their taunting jibes behind, cackling at our misery.

"Mr Higginbottom," I ventured slowly, trying to begin the conversation. "So are you going to do the running club instead of the PS Club?" He raised his head gradually as if in slow motion, and looked into my face with the biggest, cheesiest grin that flashed his teeth brightly.

"GOTCHA!" he said. "What running club? Running is for cats with black spots. I'm a gaming man myself. Anyone want to join the running club, that's fine by me, but the PS CLUB IS STILL ON," and he

cracked up laughing. "Come on boys, come on in and take a seat on the smelly mat, and I promise I won't call you kiddie widdies."

We all started to head to the mat and then Mr H coughed and paused before he spoke again. "Oh I do apologise ladies, I didn't mean to say come on boys. I meant to say, come on in boys and girls." I looked around slowly, my neck frightened to turn but my brain eager to see what he was talking about. Horror enveloped me again when I turned and saw, not one, not two, but three girls, and one of them was Elly, the new girl. Who did she think she was? I bet she put the other girls up to it for a stir.

"Someone has to tell them the PS club is just for boys," I whispered to Matthew, who only shrugged his shoulders at me. Josh overheard and butted in.

"No it's not, anyone can join." I looked at Josh in amazement, and he had that dumb, goofy look on his face again. What was going down with this kid?

"Come on girls. Roll up, roll up, come on in, don't be shy," Mr H said, like he was a circus ringmaster. But he wasn't getting any laughs from me, that's for sure. "The PS Club is open to anyone in the fifth grade. Isn't it boys?" Mr Higginbottom looked over at us with a warning look. "Come and sit down girls. These boys won't bite." *Wanna make a bet* I thought to myself.

Elly took a seat next to Nigel. I should have known *that* was going to happen. Those two were probably going to gang up together. Sophie and Sarah took a patch of mat next to Elly on the other side. I looked around at the other boys expecting to see angry looks, but I was gobsmacked to see they were just sitting still, looking up at Mr Higginbottom, waiting for him to speak. And because there was a new person, Mr H had to bore us with all the gory details of how the PS club worked even though we already knew.

"So, since we have a new class member, I should explain why this class always has amazing school results. Every day, Elly, I set tasks that everyone must complete, and set criteria that everyone must reach. At the end of the day those who make it, get a choice out of my green bucket. They can either have a raffle ticket or they can have a chocolate bar." Elly put up her hand and Mr Higginbottom nodded.

"I don't eat chocolate, so a raffle ticket would be awesome." Ok I'd heard enough. Like, seriously, who doesn't eat chocolate? Not only was this girl rough and tough, she was weird. The next thing she'd probably say was that she couldn't eat candy or cookies either.

"Oh dear," Mr H said. "That's no good. How do you survive without chocolate? Do you have extra candy instead?" he laughed.

"No, I don't eat candy or cookies either, but I don't mind."

SERIOUSLY! I had a sneaky suspicion this girl might have been a liar as well. No normal kid refuses to eat candy. Not on this planet anyway. Weird! Weird! Weird! I was going to have to keep an eye on her, especially if she was teaming up with Nigel. I had a nasty feeling they were up to something. Well I would be ready and waiting for them.

9. The PS Club RULES!

Mr Higginbottom continued telling Elly all about the PS club and how the eight people with the most raffle tickets on Friday got to play PlayStation all afternoon. Her eyes lit up like a fire cracker on the fourth of July as he explained the rules.

"Now Elly, this may sound like a lot of fun, but my students work very hard to get a raffle ticket. It doesn't come easy. They get nearly top marks, and there's absolutely NO mucking around, is there Matthew?" He looked directly at Matthew with his eyebrows doing a funny dance sort of thing. Matthew returned the look with a sheepish gaze, knowing he often ruined his chances by doing dumb things like pea shooting at girls and putting gum on their chairs, farting under his arm, and talking in class. Once he even put a lizard in Sophie's desk and made her squeal hysterically. It was the only thing he'd done wrong and he met all the criteria that day, but Mr H wouldn't let him get a raffle ticket and he missed out on the PS Club that week.

Each day at a quarter to three, Mr Higginbottom gets out his big, black book and checks who has completed all the work for the day, and who has met the criteria. Then he always makes a big announcement in a really silly voice.

"Ok kiddie widdies, grade fivey wiveys." And then he quickly changes his tone to army sergeant style. "The Criteria for the day is as follows. ......" Then he would talk about the three or four things we had to achieve that day.

Number 1. Blah blah blah about Maths.

Number 2. More Blah blah blah, usually about English.

Number 3. Blah blah blah spelling, spelling, spelling.

Then he would say something about good behavior. It was always so exciting to wait and hear whether your name would be called out or not. I was *always* on the list. I've never been one to get into trouble, but when the PS Club was created, I made sure I was the biggest goody goody this side of the moon so I didn't miss out.

Everybody that meets the criteria gets to choose from his big green bucket. You can either choose a chocolate bar or a raffle ticket. A raffle ticket is a gateway to gamers Heaven because it goes straight into the red bucket for the big draw on Friday. The eight kids with the most raffle tickets on Friday get to play PS3 all afternoon during class time in the computer room. Mr Higginbottom brings the PS 3's with him.

It's so insane. I can't believe how awesome my school is. I can't believe how awesome Mr H is, and I'm so glad he is back. I was so eager to hear what the new changes were going to be. Maybe he would have a PS4 in his brief case. I had my own PS4 from a prize I won at Movie World but it would be sick as to play PS4 at school.

"So kiddie widdies, would you like to hear the good news or the bad news?" he continued.

WOW! I was starting to think this was 'Good news/Bad news day' or something. It was some sort of national conspiracy. You couldn't have some good news without being trashed on by some bad news.

Everyone yelled out that they wanted the good news, but Mr H decided he would start with the bad news. So why did he asked us in the first place?

"Ok, I think I'll get the little problem over with first. Actually, there is no problem, just a little change that you might not be too excited about. As we all know very well, we are extremely lucky that the school permits us to play PlayStation during school hours. In fact we are highly privileged, and it took a long time for me to convince them of the educational benefits."

"I wish he would hurry up and spill his guts," I whispered to Matthew, who was sitting in front of me.

"Yeah, I know," he said over his shoulder, but Josh, who was always Mr Perfect, gave us the evil eye, making sure we remained quiet. I cheekily poked my tongue out at him, knowing Mr H couldn't see me.

"The truth is, I'm afraid to say, that the school board has decided that playing PlayStation 3 during school hours every week, although it has done no harm, is in fact, no longer permissible." I looked from Matthew to Josh and back to Mr Higginbottom. Josh looked disappointed, Mr H looked sad, Matthew had a blank face and I was totally confused, because I had absolutely no clue what the word 'permissible' meant. But I wasn't going to be dumb enough to admit it, so I just sat there, looking like a stunned mullet. I glanced back at Matthew who still had a look on his face as though the lights were on, but nobody was home. Maybe he didn't know its meaning either.

I started to panic when I realised how miserable some of the kids looked, and Mr Higginbottom continued to answer questions.

"You mean, they won't let us play anymore?" Josh asked, his voice cracking with disbelief. It was then that I realised the horror of the situation. They wouldn't allow us to do it! The school board wouldn't allow us to do it!

Who did they think they were?

All of a sudden, I felt a massive attack of missiles soaring through the sky, exploding in all directions into smithereens, nose-diving into my heart, and blasting it into a thousand jagged pieces, as the dreadful truth of the PS club hit me like a bomb.

This could not be happening!

10. More Good News and Bad News

"Hang on, hang on. Don't get your knickers in a knot. Don't jump the gun." I pictured in my head, someone running round in knotted underwear trying to jump over a gun. Gee Mr Higginbottom could say some funny things. I laughed to myself, but my laughter was quickly silenced as he went on. "There is good news to follow remember."

We all waited, dumbstruck, for Mr Higginbottom to continue. "As I said, there is good news too, and the good news is……. there's no more running club!" He paused, waiting for our reaction, then began laughing to himself awkwardly, realising his little joke hadn't been such a hit. "Ok so there's more good news as I promised. Because the PS club made everyone work so hard, and behave so well in my class, the principal and the board are willing to allow the club to continue every *second* Friday." There were some groans of disappointment but mainly a lot of relieved sighs coming from the boys. The girls just sat there quietly taking everything in. "Unfortunately," he continued, "we won't be able to play during school time. They believe it takes up too much of valuable learning time." I groaned simultaneously with Matthew, and even Josh started to whinge a bit. It really seemed like all bad news, bad news and more bad news, with just a little bit of good news sprinkled on top.

"Hang on, hang on," he continued, "before you all start whining like a group of alley cats terrorizing sewer rats, I do have some reeeeeeaaally good news stuffed way down here deep in my pocket." He dived his hand down into his trouser pocket and pulled out a scrunched up handkerchief. "Oh no hang on, that's just a snotty hanky." He laughed again. His humor was so weird, but we all laughed and it broke the tension. "All right, do you really want to know what the good news is?"

"Yes," a few of us said impatiently.

"I can't hear you," Mr Higginbottom sang, like he was the royal goose in a pantomime.

"YES!" We all roared loudly, getting really annoyed.

"Well," he began, getting down on his knees onto the mat next to us. "You remember what a cool dude my brother is? He's the guy who owns a gaming store, my dream job." There were cheerful nods all around, as we remembered how his brother donated two awesome PlayStation games at the start of the year for the PlayStation playoffs competition. I won the games, but I gave them to nasty Nigel who was the runner-up. Yep, believe me, that's what I did, but that's a long story. He didn't remain appreciative for too long that's for sure. Maybe it was because I didn't really get excited about his request to be his best buddy.

I scanned my head around the room looking at all the boys, and trying to avoid looking in the girl's direction. Everyone was starting to look more pleased as the conversation finally got a little more exciting. I couldn't wait to hear what Mr H had to say next.

11. Let the Gaming Begin

Mr H continued, "my brother, Dave, was so inspired when he heard what fun we had last time with the PlayStation playoffs, and how it encouraged everyone to work so hard. He was also incredibly touched by you Rino donating your prize to the runner up, Nigel." I gleamed inside as Mr H looked towards me with an approving smile, as my cheeks burned red on the outside.

"So," he continued, almost beaming like a light sabre, "he has decided that he would love to donate, another two games to yet another PlayStation 3 competition." There were stunned looks followed by excited gasps and frenzied chatter as we all digested the amazing news.

"What are the games?" Nigel blurted out.

"When do we start?" added Jacob.

"Will it be the same rules?" someone else queried. The questions poured in on top of each other until Mr H raised his hands up.

"Whoaaa. Hold your horses." Another weird expression. "Too many questions at once. It's like playing a game of twenty questions in a record breaking two seconds. Now, Nigel, your question first. The prizes will not be two games but a voucher to get two games of your choice. So this time, they could be Xbox games, PS games, Nintendo games, whatever your gaming hearts desire. You might even like to get Barbie Wild Horse Rescue or Dora the Explorer Saves the Kingdom," he said cheekily. It bothered me how Mr H even knew those games existed.

"Cool!" Matthew exclaimed, turning around to shine his pearly whites at me.

"Awesome!" Jacob and Josh said together. "Yeah but not Barbie or Dora. That's not awesome," Josh giggled.

"Yeah baby," Nigel said, trying to sound like Austin Powers. "I'm gonna get the new Skylanders Supercharger."

"No, what about Elder Scrolls V," suggested Jay.

"Oh yeah, cool man," agreed Jacob.

"Nah! That's old news. I've got that. I want Skylanders Superchargers too," Peter said.

"Hey, I got the new swap force Skylanders character pack last week," Matthew said gloating. He was always getting awesome presents from his dad when his dad went away for work.

"Tell someone who cares," snarled Nigel. He was really on a roll of nastiness lately. Maybe he was trying to impress the newbie with his bullying tactics.

Everybody kept calling out what they would like to win. I was secretly hoping that I would be able to get the new 'Star Wars Battlefront' but I didn't want to jinx it by telling everybody.

"Righteo then cool cats, go out and enjoy your lunch, and don't forget to eat healthily. Tomorrow will be the first day that we will begin. Every day at a quarter to three, I will go through the criteria and see who gets a raffle ticket or a chocolate bar. But I won't be counting them until next week as we now have two weeks to wait." Again there were disgruntled murmurs as the truth sunk in that we would be playing only every fortnight. It seemed like an overwhelming amount of time to wait to see if you made it into the club.

"Any more questions?" he added.

"Can we choose the game we play in the comps like last time?"

"Der! Of course we can," replied Nigel.

"Well actually, no, Nigel, you can't," Mr Higginbottom stated firmly. "I will be choosing the game, and you will all be playing the same game, so it's fair."

There were a few surprised looks again, but most of the kids took the news well. Then the new girl put up her hand. I couldn't help thinking how bold she was asking questions when she wasn't a part of the group.

"Mr Higginbottom, what happens if you don't have a PS 3 at home? Will it affect your chances?"

"Well, I suggest you beg, borrow or steal one, because, practicing *will* make a difference," Mr Higginbottom laughed. I didn't think it was such a good suggestion to put the idea of stealing into her head. She didn't really look like a trustworthy person.

My mom always says, "don't judge a book by its cover," which means that you don't judge the way a person is by the way they might look. But my dad always says, "go with your guts," which sounds gross. Going with your gooey, squishy guts can't be fun. But Dad said it meant, to believe in what your gut reaction or first thoughts were about someone. Well I was going with my guts on this one. Elly the new kid was bad news. I could tell, and I could sense danger ahead with that girl.

12. Number 1 Rule : No Girls Allowed

On the way home that afternoon, Josh, Matthew and I couldn't stop talking about the PS competition and trying to guess what game Mr H would choose.

"Someone's got to tell the new girl that no girls are allowed in the club," I said, fishing for agreement. Matthew was the first one to disappoint me when he looked up frowning.

"What? How come? I've never heard that rule before. Mr Higginbottom let them stay."

"Well he was probably just trying to be kind. But we can't let them in. They'll ruin it. We don't want stinky girls in the club, do we?"

Josh replied in their defence which made me fume. I swear I could feel little smoke puffs coming out of my ears as he stuck up for the girls. "Why not? Who cares whether they're in the club or not? What difference does it make?" he said defensively.

I couldn't believe what I was hearing. "Because they'll wreck it that's why. They'll probably bring their dull Dora dolls and talk about makeup and Instagram, and won't even play games. And if they do play games they'll be hopeless anyway."

Matthew laughed out loud, and as he did, he let a big whopper shoot out of his behind, causing him to turn a bright shade of red. "Oh holy cow. I did NOT mean to do that one."

"Yeah right Mattie. Like you didn't mean the last seven hundred farts you've done this year," Josh answered him.

"I didn't." Matthew actually looked embarrassed. "I was just laughing so hard at the thought of that new girl playing with Dora the explorer. Somehow I don't think she's the type."

"I don't think any of the girls in our grade play with dolls, not Dora dolls anyway," Josh laughed.

"Can we stop talking about girls and dolls please? It's really not my favorite subject to talk about," I pleaded.

"What's wrong Rino? Are you scared the girlies might beat you?" Matthew teased, as he whacked me on the shoulders.

"Get off it!" I said, whacking him back. "As if! No-one's gonna beat me, let alone a girl!"

"Haha, you wish. Dream on. I'm gonna blitz you this time," Josh pumped out, still laughing. "Hey, who wants to meet on Minecraft later?"

"I can't. It's not my night for computer time. Unless Mom's gone to work, then I can sneak a bit in." Normally I don't like to be deceitful, but my mom has all these stupid, unreasonable rules that really don't allow for adequate time on gaming platforms like –

No computer time unless its Wednesday.

No PlayStation unless it's the weekend.

No iPad for Lisa after 8.30, even though she has it every day. (Grrrr)

No cookies after tea,

No cookies before tea,

No candy during the week.

It's a wonder she lets us breathe whenever we want to. One day she'll probably make up a rule about what time we're allowed to poop, and how much loo paper we can use.

"Ok, well if you get on, I'll see you there. I'm going to build a Skyrim style castle. It's gonna be epic," Josh announced.

"Yeah might see ya on Minecraft Josh," I replied.

"Yeah I'll be there," Matthew called out, as Josh took off towards his street.

As I looked up, I could see Nigel and Elly walking ahead together. Nigel's street was close to mine (unfortunately). "Be careful with that new girl Mattie," I said quietly. "I think she's bad news. I think she put Nigel up to tripping you today."

"What? Nah. She came up to me when we were playing Red Rover and asked if I was ok. Said she was really embarrassed about what he did." My mouth dropped open as he spoke. I had to slam it shut again or a swarm of flies would have rushed in.

"What? I don't believe you."

"It's true."

"Something's going down man. Why would a girl come up and say sorry for someone else's bullying?"

"Dunno. Maybe she felt bad."

"Be careful Mattie. Be very careful. Oh don't look now. They're coming towards us. Stay cool."

"What do you mean stay cool? I'm always cool. When am I never cool?" Mattie joked.

"Only like every day, 24 /7," I laughed.

"Hey, I'll drop a gas bomb on you for that."

"Yeah right," but I took off, out of his way just in case, intending to run right passed Nigel and his girlfriend and pretend not to notice them. Strangely enough, as I scurried past them, they didn't even seem to notice me, but when they got to Matthew, they stopped and started to talk to him so I casually went back to see what they were up to. As much as I like Matthew, sometimes he has the brains of a gold fish, and with Nigel being one of the biggest sharks around, Matthew could get himself into a lot of trouble. A shark with a catfish supporting him, versus a gold fish, just wasn't a fair game.

Nigel looked sheepishly toward Matthew and rolled his eyes as if he didn't want to do something. As I approached the troublesome two, I saw Elly give Nigel a poke in the ribs. Boy was she game, poking a bully. Nigel went to speak, but Matthew interrupted them first. "Hi guys," he said. I'm not sure what he was hoping to achieve by being nice to them.

"Hi," said Elly. "What's your name?"

"Matthew, some of my friends call me Mattie."

"Can I call you Mattie?" Elly asked. Mathew was dumbstruck. I'm not sure whether he'd ever talked to a girl before and even though she was a tom boy, he was still hashing it up pretty bad.

"Yeah sure. What's yours?"

"Aw der," Nigel quipped. "Like, it's ELLY. She told us in class," he said, with a slow drawn out tone as if speaking to a toddler.

"I know that, I meant her surname, know-it-all."

Elly took a big sigh and looked around at me and said, "Gross." I knew she was a mean girl. She hardly even knew me and she was calling me gross.

"Gee, thanks," I snapped, insulted by her name calling, as Nigel started laughing. I raised my eye brows at Matthew.

"No I'm not calling *you* that. It's my name, Elly Grace Gross." I started to laugh a bit. I tried to hold it in because I know people can't help their names, but my mouth kept twitching, giving the game away. I could see Matthew was doing his best to remain polite as well. Nigel of course laughed evilly, enjoying the girl's misfortune.

"Go on, laugh as hard as you want," Elly stated plainly. "Make up all the names you want. I've been called it *all* before, gross out, gross burger, gross smell, grossness, grossed out big time, and even, smelly Elly with the skinny belly."

Elly stood there smirking as she rattled off all the names, while Nigel nearly peed himself laughing, and Matthew and I looked at each other embarrassed. I actually felt bad that the new girl would think I would be so cruel as to call her names. No matter what I thought of her, name calling was not my kind of thing. I hadn't even given her surname a second thought because I used to have a teacher in second grade called Mrs Gross, who was awesome, so I was used to it.

"Well actually, I didn't even think about your surname," I began timidly, unsure as to whether she was going to bite my head off or not. "I was just having a little chuckle to myself because your initials spell EGG." Nigel laughed even harder. He was so immature, but

59

Matthew remained straight faced. I think he was afraid she might cut his head off.

Elly looked shocked and was lost for words. "Oh!" was all she could say. Then there was this really uncomfortable pause before she found her tongue again. "Well anyway, Nigel wanted to say something to Matthew." Nigel was still rolling around the ground, laughing his head off in a very loud way trying to get attention by laughing hysterically.

"Do I?" he questioned, looking at her confused. She gave him a stern look and he rolled his eyes yet again. "Oh yeah, I do, apparently." He looked at Matthew. "Sorry for tripping you over today. It was an accident, well sort of an accident. My leg just has this habit of sticking up when someone is running past, and it's a hard habit to get out of." He turned to Elly as if to say, 'are you satisfied?'

"That's ok," said Matthew. "Just don't do it again."

"Who me?" Nigel replied cheekily. I didn't know what to make of the situation. There I was, walking home trying to mind my own business, and am confronted by Nigel, acting super brainless, and the new girl acting super nice, making Nigel apologise. Alarm bells were ringing as my danger radar gremlin was starting to work overtime as I thought about Elly and Nigel, and what plan they were hatching.

13. Sorry is such a Big Word

When I got home, I was disappointed to see Mom wasn't at work, so I couldn't have any secretive Minecraft time. Mom and Lisa were busy in the garage organising a yard sale. Lisa was saving up money for something secret, and she'd come up with this brainy idea that she could sell all our worldly possessions and get a couple of dollars for them. So I decided to stay out of her way as she was in a price tagging frenzy and I hated yard sales.

"How was school?" Mom called out.

"Yeah good, but bad. Mr Higginbottom is back," and when I spoke, it dawned on me that I hadn't even asked him how his Mother was. I felt really bad, but I'd been too excited about the news of the PlayStation competition.

Mom walked down the stairs. "Oh yes I heard. I bumped into Josh's mom at the market. That was very sad about his Mother." My heart stopped beating momentarily as I pondered over what she'd said.

"What, you mean sad about her being sick?" I asked hopefully, not wanting to entertain any other thoughts.

"Well no," Mom began hesitantly. "She lost her battle with her illness a couple of weeks ago, which is why Mr Higginbottom had extra time off."

I felt a tear invade my eye socket and I suddenly felt terrible, like a spoiled brat who was worried only about themselves. I had been excited all day about the PS club and obsessed with the new girl trashing the club, that I hadn't even given a second thought to Mr Higginbottom. I felt about as low as the scum that floats on a gold fish pond. Actually I felt even lower than that. I felt like the larvae that sucks on the scum on a pond. Then my thoughts of scum suddenly turned to worry, as I panicked as to what I would say to Mr Higginbottom the next day. I wouldn't know what to say. I would just ignore it. That would be the best plan.

"Did he say anything about it today?" Mom queried.

"No."

"Well did you ask him?"

"No."

"Perhaps you should take him a card tomorrow, and say how sorry you are."

"What? Mom, no. I can't say anything to him about it. I wouldn't know what to say. I'd probably make a fool of myself and say something stupid." What was my Mom thinking? Ten year old boys don't talk about dead people. I started to panic at the thought of it.

"Ryan, when someone loses a loved one, it's nice to know that other people care, and if you don't say something to him, or acknowledge it in some way, how will Mr Higginbottom know that you are thinking of him and his loss?" My mom had a good point, (as usual). She always has these really bad ideas but somehow they always seem to make sense in the end. But the thought of it scared the willies out of me.

"Mom I won't know what to say," I repeated.

"Rino, even if you just utter one word, 'sorry' I'm sure it will mean a lot to Mr Higginbottom to know someone cares. I'll get you a card later that you can take to school." I decided even if it killed me, I would just walk up to him in the morning and say, "sorry about your mom." Later on that evening I would practice in the bathroom mirror.

Lisa came in and butted in on my thoughts. At least she stopped me from thinking too much about Mr H's mom. She was wearing white shorts that went all the way up to her neck, but hardly covered her butt cheeks. She looked ridiculous. I think she calls them her high waisted shorts, but to me, they looked more like low necked shorts. They had 'Number One Princess' in pink glitter on her behind. She's

about as number one princess as the ugliest toad in the royal pond. But it doesn't help that Dad always calls her princess. Eewghy Spewy.

What is it about girls?

"Can I sell your old teddy bears?" she asked in an out of character pleasant tone. Usually she speaks to me like I am a snail standing in her way.

"What, no," I said. "You can't get rid of those."

"Oh you're such a baby. As if you still play with teddy bears. Or do you, little baby? Goo goo gaa ga," she taunted.

"I DO NOT PLAY WITH THEM!" I shouted back. "People gave them to me when I was a kid."

"Yes Lisa," Mom added. "They have sentimental value because family members gave them to him when he was a baby." Wow, Mom was sticking up for me for a change. Usually it's Lisa who gets everything her way, and Mom usually sticks up for her. Even if Lisa was to pellet me with hail fire and a hand grenade, Mom would probably say I deserved it.

"Are you feeling ok Mom?" I asked, hoping she wouldn't realize I was being cheeky.

"Of course, why?"

"Ah, no reason."

"But Mom, they're all grotty and yukky and the ears are all chewed up from when Ryan sucked on them last year," Lisa pleaded.

"I DID NOT. That was where Pugsley chewed it." Pugsley was our old dog. He had a habit of chewing on everything but his own toys when he was a puppy.

"Well if that's true Lisa, then no-one would want to buy them, so it's pointless putting them out for sale. End of story." Mom was firm in the way she spoke. I was having a silent party inside because she was sticking up for me. It was a rare occasion. "Right Lisa, back to the garage, and Rino, onto your homework. I've left a fruit salad for you on the bench."

"Has it got cream and ice cream on it Mom?"

"Yes of course it has Ryan. IN YOUR DREAMS!" I don't know why my mother has to be such a health nut. I'm sure she was a rabbit in a previous life. We have so much stuff to eat out of a cabbage patch.

As I left the room to go and get my super healthy fruit salad, Mom called out to me, "don't forget to do your super spelling list." I think Mom has this secret desire to be a teacher, and for me to become this super smart human being. It's not enough for her that we do spelling and English at school, she has to make me do extra. After I do all my homework every night, I have to look for hard words and write their definitions down, and then she tests me at the end of the week. BORING!! And PSYCHO!!

"Yes Mom," I called back in a slow drawl, and I went upstairs and left them to their yard sale planning. I didn't want to have anything to do with it. I told Lisa that she wasn't to go anywhere near the stuff in my bedroom, but she could have whatever she wanted that was in the garage, as long as she gave me the money for it. She said she had to have commission for doing all the hard work. "Whatever," was my reply. For the fifty cents I'd get for some dumb toy, I'd probably have to give half to her in commission. So by the end, if I was lucky, I might have enough money to buy a packet of candy. Whoopee do!

I trudged upstairs with my fruit salad, and got ready to do my homework. I thought about having a quick session on Minecraft while my mom was busy in the garage, but I thought about how dishonest it was, and decided not to. Being dishonest was not one of my favorite things to do, but occasionally I weakened, and had a couple of computer games when I wasn't supposed to. Like when Lisa torments me about something, and the only thing I can do to get over it, is build a nether reactor or something cool like that.

I went to bed that night excited about the first day of the red and green bucket challenge and trying to get a raffle ticket. As I drifted off to sleep, I wondered what game Mr H was going to choose for the competition. It would be insane if he chose a game I had already blitzed.

At least I had an advantage over some of the others. Even though I won a PS 4 at Movie World earlier in the year, I still had my PlayStation 3 somewhere, so I could drag it out and practice, whereas some of the boys only had Xboxes or PS 4's.

My hyper brain struggled to fall asleep, and I tossed and turned from side to side, punching the pillow and kicking the sheets off. Finally I lost all sense of time and place and found myself in one of those mad Minecraft dreams I'd been having recently. This time the dream wasn't clear. All I can remember were zombies and pig men all over the place running around attacking each other, but they were trapped in another world. It was the setting of Skyrim. Then one of them curdled, "CEASE FIRE," and they all dropped to their knees, and sat down at TV sets. Another zombie yelled out, "let the games begin," and they all started wrestling with remote controls while battling each other in a PlayStation game. Weird! Weird! Weird!

66

I woke suddenly at the sound of my own shrieking laughter. Seeing the zombies play PlayStation had been so funny I must have laughed so hard that I woke myself up. Sometimes I fart so hard in my sleep that I wake myself up, but I'd never woken up laughing before. As I struggled to get back to sleep, it dawned on me that I didn't get to see my Dad that evening, as he was late home, and I still didn't know what *his* good news was, (or his bad news).

I looked at the dogs sleeping on the end of my bed. They looked very comfortable and cute, even if my toes do get squashed, and I get pins and needles.

I really wanted to know what Dad's news was, but if I moved, I would disturb the dog's sleeping peacefully. I could find out the answer in the morning, if Dad didn't leave too early. In the meantime I crossed my fingers hoping the news would be really good and I struggled off to sleep.

14. News? What News?

When my alarm clock rang the next morning, I pressed the silence button twice before I dragged myself out of bed. I still had my old Thomas the Tank clock and the snooze button was right in the middle of his nose, so every time I pressed it, it was like I was punching him in the nose.

I was about to open my computer when I remembered Dad's news, so I quickly mustered some energy and bounded downstairs before I missed him. Half way down, I jumped on the stair rail and slid the rest of the way down. Mom hates me doing that, but that's only because she's old and doesn't realize how awesome it is. "Incoming," I called, as I landed on the floor with a thud.

The two dogs came bounding up to me, wagging their tales in a tail wagging frenzy. They jumped up and down all over me, licking my legs and trying to slobber over my face when I bent down to hug them.

I loved looking after Maxi and Tess, and the thought of losing them always made rebel streams of water gush out of my eye sockets (yeah alright; crying, sooking, blubbing, whatever you want to call it). Yet I knew the time was getting close because their owner Bob was out of hospital. I hated thinking about it. They had become so much a part of the family since we met Bob at the caravan park and he'd had a heart attack. I wished Dad would offer to buy them from Bob. Every night when I went to bed, I prayed that we would somehow get to keep them; that a miracle would happen.

I could hear Dad clattering with his keys so I knew he was probably leaving. "**Daaaaaaad,**" I screamed catching him fleeing out the front door.

"Morning bud. Have a good day at school. Got to go, I'm running late." He hurried off down the driveway before I had a chance to stop him. NO! This was not going to happen again. I needed to know pronto what his secret news was.

"Daaaaaaad!" I screamed, chasing him into the car in my pyjamas. "Wait up! What's the news?"

He stared at me blankly. "What news?" Oh man. Was I the only person in this family that had a memory?

"The news! You said yesterday morning that you had some good news and some bad news, and then you raced off, and I'm not letting you race off again without telling me. DAD!!"

"Oh that. Oh don't worry, nothing exciting," and he slammed the door shut, locked it and turned on the engine whilst poking his tongue out at me cheekily.

"Daaaaaad," I squawked again, like a cockatoo gripping onto the side of the door. I had these visions of Dad driving down the road with me holding on tight, legs flying everywhere as I struggled to hold on. I valued my life better than that and I still wanted to play so many PlayStation games as well as win the PS comp, so I gave up, disappointed, and let go of the car. Dad gave me a cheeky wink as he reversed the car, and spun quickly down the road.

I kicked the gravel with my bare foot in anger. "DOH!" I said to myself as I realized how much it hurt. I was looking down at the blood I'd drawn on my big toe when I heard a car approaching. To my surprise, I saw Dad had done a u-turn and was coming back past the house. But oddly he wasn't stopping. As he slowed down, he put his window down and yelled something out to me, then sped off.

I strained my ears to hear what he'd said. At first I thought I was mistaken, but then I realized what he'd said as I replayed it in my mind. My heart started racing, my eyes popped open wide and my body started jumping up and down in a frenzy, as I shouted, "Yippee," like a big dumb kid. I quickly looked around to make sure no one had seen me do my dork dance in my Thomas pyjamas. Embarrassment big time.

15. Is it True?

I bounded inside shrieking at the top of my voice to Mom. If the neighbors weren't awake, they would have been rudely awaken by my screeching. "Mom! Is it true? Is it true?" I was running around looking for her madly, and unfortunately I bumped into this ghastly looking creature that resembled a swamp monster surfacing out of the deep. Its fur stood up in fuzzy strands around a face that drooped sourly to the ground.

"Watch where you are going and get out of my way," it demanded in a sour tone. "And is what true?" Lisa was always a little bit zombie-like before she had her breakfast. Mom secretly told me to always keep out of her way until she'd had her cereal and juice in the mornings.

And she was right! Lisa definitely wasn't a pretty sight

when she'd just gotten up, and she definitely wasn't very charming either.

"Nothing!" I replied. "And if you're going to speak to me like that, you can mind your own bees wax."

"Oh seriously, you're such a knob noob. Who wants to know anyway?"

"You do, that's why you asked me," I fired back.

"Well I probably already know anyway," she smirked and went off to the kitchen. She was probably right. I was always the last to know everything in this house. There was a definite imbalance of importance round here. The younger you were, the less you got to find out, and the less you got to make decisions, and the less you got to go places, and the less awesome things you got and the less............. Yeah I could go on forever, you get the picture. It sucks being the youngest.

But at that moment, I didn't care. I was so excited. I kept screaming to Mom, and she kept ignoring me. Finally I found her in the bedroom having a wrestle with the hoover. I think I heard her talking to it too, and she wasn't saying nice things. She looked up at me with an irritated face.

"Oh this hoover is driving me mad. I've seen more sucking power in a gold fish. I literally have to pick up the dust and shove it down its nostril for it to get anywhere."

"Mom, what are you on about?" I laughed.

"This hoover. It doesn't work. Never mind. What's wrong?" I got all excited again as I asked Mom.

"So is it true? What Dad said?"

"What are you talking about? What Dad said. How do I know what Dad said?" Mom had a cheeky grin so I suspected she knew exactly what was on my mind.

"Are the dogs going to stay? Mom, are they?"

"Well, yes it does look like they might be here for a while longer yet," she grinned.

"YES! YES! YES!" I punched the air with a powerful force on each word. I raced around the house like a superhero on a mission. I went into a complete frenzy lost in another world of excitement, fighting zombies and bad guys.

I drew an imaginary light sabre from my waist and attacked the zombie in the kitchen. She looked at me weirdly. I raced after the dogs and beckoned them to join my troupe. "Let's get her," I commanded the animals. "We are indestructible. We are heroes. Let's fight the enemy together. Let's get her boys," and we bombarded the enemy sitting at the breakfast table in a state of shock.

"Mooooooom," the enemy shouted. "Ryan's gone all weird again. Help Mom!" she shouted. "What are you on, you stupid dumb head?"

"LISA!" That's enough. Do not use ghastly expressions like that about another human being, particularly your brother." Mom had walked in just as Lisa was mouthing off at me and she was in trouble. I sniggered smugly. One point to me. About time too. I was always the one getting into trouble.

"But you should have seen what he was doing. He was attacking me violently."

Mom looked at me for answers.

"I did nothing," I lied, looking innocent. "I was just having a bit of fun because the dogs are allowed to stay."

"What? The dogs are staying?" Lisa forgot all about her anger towards me when she heard the news. "How come no-one told me? Why am I always the last one to find things out? Oh Maxi, come here," she called to the little dog with a sudden change of tone. "You're going to stay with your Mommy. I can't believe it. You don't have to go back to the mean old man."

"Lisa! That's enough. Bob is a lovely old man. It's just that he's not going to be well enough to go back to his own house for quite some time, so he'll be staying with his sister in the flat. So it won't be forever, but it will be a while longer yet," Mom instructed. Lisa and I both went chasing the dogs around the house together in uncontrollable excitement.

It was the best piece of news I'd had since the return of Mr Higginbottom the day before and his announcement about a new PlayStation competition. It had been an awesome twenty four hours with two super insane, wildly incredible and absolutely unbelievable bits of news. It was such a bummer that it all had to be trashed by Elly the new girl wanting to hijack the PS club with Nigel.

16. It's Cool to be Kind

Before I went to school, Mom handed me a card. "What's this for?" I asked.

"It's a sympathy card for Mr Higginbottom," she replied.

"What's a sympathy card?"

"It's a card you give to someone you know when a loved one passes away."

"Away, where? Passes where? What do you mean?" I asked, somewhat confused. Mom looked a bit uneasy.

"You know, when someone dies. Because Mr Higginbottom's mom died, you can give him a sympathy card to show your respect."

"Oh, well why didn't you just say, when someone dies? I would have known what you were talking about."

"Well, sometimes people find it difficult to say the word 'die'. It's nicer to use a softer expression like, 'passes away', don't you think?" I looked at Mom blankly. I really had no idea why people wouldn't just say the real word.

But I had more important things on my mind, like, what I was actually going to say to Mr Higginbottom when I gave him the card. I think Mom could see my nervousness because she said, "now all you have to say is 'sorry to hear about your Mom'. You don't need to get all worried." She was right. I was very worried. I thought he might think I was nosy or stupid or something.

I remembered I had a stash of chocolate bars in my cupboard. I take after Mom. She hides candy and chocolate from us in her secret stashes, but when she's not looking, sometimes I build my own secret stash in my secret box in my secret drawer in the desk.

I thought it might cheer Mr Higginbottom up if he had a chocolate bar given to him. I know when I feel sad, chocolate always cheers me up. I quickly wrote on the card. I couldn't think of anything to say, so I just wrote, *To Mr Higginbottom, from Ryan*. The card had its own words in it anyway.

When I got to school, Matthew, Josh and Jacob were all hanging round the front, playing handball. We still had ten minutes until class so they wanted me to play with them, but I just wanted to get the passing away card thing over before anyone could see. It would be embarrassing if other kids saw me give it to him.

"Nah, I've got to give something to Mr H. I'll see you in class," I said as I scurried off.

"Give what to Mr Higginbottom?" Matthew, the sticky beak asked, chasing after me.

"Nothing. Boring stuff."

"What?" he persisted. "You want me to blow chunks at you out of my butt cheeks?"

"MATTHEW. GET LOST," I said laughing, knowing he was joking, even though he started to turn his rear end towards me. "It's nothing, just a dumb old card that my mom wanted me to give him."

"What for?"

"Didn't your Mom ever teach you it was rude to be a sticky nose?"

"Nuh! She just taught me that it was rude to have secrets," he chuckled.

"It's not a secret!" I said getting frustrated. "It's just a dumb old card 'cos his mom passed away."

"Where did she go away to?" It was good to know Matthew was just as dumb as I was, even if he was nosey.

"She went to heaven. She died. That's what passed away means dumb nut. It's just a card for him to say sorry."

"Oh cool," he replied. "I mean, it's not cool, about his Mom. It's cool that you got him a card. Can I sign it?" I was a bit shocked that Mattie would want to sign it, because I thought he would think I was stupid.

"Yeah ok." As he was signing it, Josh and Jacob got in on the act and wanted to as well. Before I knew it, there were about ten other sticky beaks signing the card. And guess what?

77

They all thought I was real cool for thinking of it. I suppose Mom does have some good ideas sometimes, even if she does nag a bit.

When I gave the card and chocolate to Mr Higginbottom before the bell went, his eyes went all sort of fuzzy and glassy looking. Maybe it was because he wasn't wearing his glasses and he couldn't read the words properly. At first I thought he didn't like it, because he looked really sad, but then he gently said, "that is one of the kindest things any of my students have ever done. And I've been teaching for a very long time as you can tell by my grey hairs." I was quietly chuffed that I was the first student to think of it, even if it was Mom's idea.

I didn't have to say much at all either. The card said it all for me, and then Mr H spoke while I was summoning up my courage to think of something to say. I realised it was a really nice idea of Mom's to give him a card. I think I'll do that from now on for everyone who has someone that passes away then dies.

"I'm going to put it right here on my desk next to the other card I got today."

My ears pricked up at his statement. "You got another card today?"

"Yes, the new girl Elly must have heard about my mother and she brought me a card, and some flowers from her garden."

My blood started to boil. What was this new girl up to? Not only did she have the makings of being a bully, clearly, she was also very deceptive and cunning. It was obvious she was going to try and suck up to the teacher so she could get into the PlayStation club. She was probably even hoping for a bonus raffle ticket because she gave the teacher a card. I was going to have to put a stop to her conniving pranks.

17. Bad Jokes on the Smelly Mat

At the end of an amazing day, we all gathered on the mat to wait and see who was going to get a raffle ticket or a chocolate bar. It was like someone had turned a good behavior switch on all the kids. Imagine that! I could become really rich if I could invent a good behavior button for children. Parents from all around the world would be queuing up to buy one.

Because the PS club was back on again, all the trouble makers were acting really good, the average kids were acting even better, and the goody goodies just kept on being goody goodies. I wasn't really a goody goody, but when the PS club was on, I definitely acted like one, even if it was fake.

Mr Higginbottom put on one of his crazy voices, and told us all to sit on the mat. "Come on all you kiddy widdies, come on down to this delightful, smelly mat and sit as quietly as a cat. You know the cat who sat on the smelly mat. Be that smelly cat everyone." He laughed at himself, and looked around at all the blank faces.

"What......?" he said, like a teenager. Then he spoke like he was an Italian chef in a pizza joint. "You not thinka my joke iser funny? EH? Whatsa matter you?"

I couldn't help laughing along with the rest of the class. He was so crazy, but so funny. It amazed me how he could still crack jokes and be all happy just after his Mom had died. But maybe he just left the sad stuff at home while he came to school.

My mom told me that sometimes we had to do that. Sometimes we just have to leave bad or sad thoughts at the door when we go somewhere, and get on with what we're doing. I thought that was probably what Mr H was doing, and maybe he was even acting up and being a little crazy to help him forget his sadness. He was such a good teacher. It made me feel a little bit gloomy and squishy in my stomach to know what he'd been through.

But those squishy mushy thoughts soon disappeared when he made the big announcement about the kids who had met all criteria.

"Now listen in folks, for those that have short term memory problems, and for the newbies here, I'm going to run over the rules of the competition. If you meet all the criteria for the day, and by the way, I won't accept any bribes in the way of chocolate, candy or money, unless of course it's over a million dollars; then I would most certainly think about it, despite it being terribly immoral, unethical, corrupt, unscrupulous, not to mention downright bad, bad, bad!"

He drew in his breath as if gasping for air. "Now, where was I?" He screwed his nose up looking confused and made his cheeks puff out like a bull frog. "I momentarily got muddled up inside my brain space. Yes, that's right. If you achieve all the criteria for today, I will allow you to take a delicacy from my precious green bucket here. Remember, one of the main criteria is that you haven't been in trouble today. You may choose a scrumptious chocolate bar, or a miserable scrap of paper in the shape of a raffle ticket. If you choose a choc bar, do not eat it in class unless you want to share it with me." He smiled cheekily. "If you choose a raffle ticket, you place it in the red bucket, and you can be proud of yourself for choosing not to rot your chompers," and he gave another cheesy grin and chomped his teeth together showing off a glistening sparkle.

Everyone looked around at each other, hoping they would be included on the list. "So, every second Friday before lunch, I will have counted the raffle tickets, and the eight people with the most will get to go into the most awesome, super dooper, phantasmagorical, PS

82

club and get to be in the competition. Now let's get down to b.b.b.b..busy business," he said with an intentional stutter. "Let's have a lookey at who has made the list in my big black book."

He opened the black book. Some kids were trying to take a peek, but he reclined away from them raising his eyebrows in mock disgust.

"Righteo, the grand criteria is……

Number one, ten out of ten for Maths this morning,

Number two, homework handed in on time,

Number three, your art piece finished, completely,

Number four, at least eight out of ten in the spelling test and

Number five, of course, is that you haven't been in trouble today."

I thought pretty hard and tried to judge whether I'd made all the criteria or not. Some boys were moaning which meant they probably knew they hadn't. My heart started ticking; waiting to see if my name was called out.

I looked over to Josh who was beaming brightly, and the new girl sitting next to him was beaming even brighter. I looked across to Matthew, but he looked about as happy as a dog getting his temperature taken by a vet. (If you don't know where they put the thermometer, ask your Mom.) I figured he might have bummed out on some of the Maths problems earlier in the day. But I was pretty sure I would be in, but then again, I wasn't sure how many I'd got wrong in the spelling test as Mr H marks them.

18. Girls everywhere.

I held my breath as he started to rattle off the names. I swear my cheeks were going blue from lack of oxygen, but I seriously forgot to breathe. Finally, he called out my name. I let out a gasp of air that had enough force to create a deathly tsunami at the local pool. Josh, too, was relieved at the sound of his name, but Matthew bombed out much to his despair.

There were only six people that achieved all the criteria despite everyone acting like goody goodies all day. He'd made it pretty tough with the Math worksheets, and the spelling words were extra hard. I felt sorry for Matthew, but I was more distressed by three of the names that Mr Higginbottom called out. THEY WERE GIRLS! And one of them was Elly with the smelly belly.

I breathed another sigh of relief when Sophie went up and chose a chocolate bar out of the green bucket. Sophie loves her chocolates, but I think she might eat a few too many. I'm pretty sure her idol is Violet Beauregarde from Charlie's Chocolate Factory. She's always chewing gum and she works hard at developing the best zits ever.

Elly followed her up to the bucket and yet another wave of relief came thundering out of my nostrils as she picked up a sugar free cherry bar and not a ticket. Sugar free, can you believe! I think I breathed out a little too hard, because some green looking particles shot out of my nose as I exhaled through the nostrils.

I looked around hoping no-one had seen the floating intrusion to the atmosphere, but when I looked back to the front, Elly had done the unimaginable. I couldn't believe it.

19. One More Time : NO GIRLS ALLOWED

For some reason, Elly had put the sugar free cherry bar back down and changed it for a raffle ticket. What was she thinking? What was the point of her getting a raffle ticket? Surely she didn't think for a moment that she would be allowed in the PS club. Didn't she get it? No girls were allowed in the club. NO GIRLS ALLOWED! Why weren't people getting the point? I needed to make a sign.

As she walked back to the mat, Grace's name was called out and to my horror, she also took a raffle ticket and put it in the red bucket. This was not a good start to the PlayStation competition. Three girls and three boys made the criteria. What sort of cool gaming session would we have if we got sissy girls in the club?

I nudged Matthew and gave him my best dumbfounded look. He just shrugged his shoulders as if he didn't care. I looked at Nigel who was smirking because he'd got a raffle ticket. I tried to catch Josh's eye, but he was staring at the new girl as she put her raffle ticket into the red bucket. Man this could not be happening!

20. Chicken Nuggets

Every day after that was a mad panic at a quarter to three as we waited for Mr H to get out his big black book and see who made the criteria for the day. And every day my name was on the list without fail. So was Joshes and Jacob's and unfortunately, so was Nigel's. Even though he'd started to go back to his bullying ways and tease kids, he was smart, and he NEVER did anything in front of the teachers, so he never got into trouble.

Matthew didn't make it every day, but I hoped he might have got enough tickets to make it into the top eight at the end of the fortnight.

He'll never learn. He's too funny for his own good. One day he got into trouble by making a fart sound under his arm in library session. He would have got away with it, except he decided to milk it, and he did another, louder one and half the class started laughing hysterically. Mrs Oldman, the librarian was determined to find out who it was, and she 'sniffed' out the culprit, even though his underarm farts don't smell. He makes up for it with his butt blasters though, that's for sure.

But that wasn't the worst news. The worst news was really bad. It was as bad as if all the PlayStation games in the world got incinerated by a deadly bomb. That would be the end of the world if that happened.

The new girl Elly had managed to slime her way round the teacher and had achieved all the criteria every day *and* the worst nightmare of all was that she chose a raffle ticket every day. Even when Grace decided to choose a chocolate bar instead of a raffle ticket, Elly still kept throwing raffle tickets into the red bucket.

I really didn't want to think about playing PS games against a girl. I would rather stick pins in my eyes and eat worms with tomato sauce. It would be such a boring, one sided flogging. She would get smashed. And it would be just plain weird having a girl sit there while we played, talking boy stuff. I probably wouldn't even feel like talking.

But the way it was going, one of us was going to have to play Elly in the first heat, and I crossed my fingers that it wouldn't be me. In fact I crossed my toes, legs, arms, eyeballs, Everything! I'd have even crossed my willy if I could.

Towards the end of the second week, Mr H went a bit crazy with the bonus tickets. He said he wanted to make the final eight an exciting draw. So every time someone did something really good or really sucky, he gave them a bonus ticket.

By Thursday afternoon, I knew I had a ticket for every day, but I didn't get any bonuses because I have this rule that it's not cool to suck up to the teachers. But there were lots of kids who didn't care and they sucked up big time by doing odd jobs. One kid even offered to go and clean up the chicken poop from the chicken coop. Mr H said since it sounded like a good start to a poem, he could have two raffle tickets if he did it.

It wasn't fair. There were going to be lots of boys in the running (and at least one girl), and we still didn't even know what game was going to be the battle ground.

21. Girls are Such Losers

As we sat on the mat and Mr Higginbottom did his silly kiddy widdy speech, I crossed my fingers and hoped that I would be in the top eight raffle ticket holders. I didn't want to think about not getting in. The thought of not hearing my name called out, and having to go out into the school yard for lunch while eight other suckers went into the computer room to play PlayStation made me barf. It was NOT going to happen

I looked around. The boys were all sitting up straight and the girls were slouching around, bored with the PlayStation stuff. Most of them thought it was really unfair that they always had to go through it. But as Mr Higginbottom reminded them, they were always pleased when they won chocolate bars. I looked over at Josh and he winked at me. I looked around at Nigel, but he was picking his nose so I quickly turned the other way in disgust. As I did, I found Elly staring straight at me smiling. Eewwgh! That was creepy.

"Good luck," she whispered in my direction, before turning to Josh and saying the same. I screwed my face up in disgust as I looked the other way, and mocked a vomiting gesture towards Matthew out of Elly's view. I wondered what she was up to, trying to be nice to us. But much to my shock, Josh returned the good luck encouragement back to her. *Traitor he was*, I thought. Wishing a *girl* good luck! I caught a glimpse of Jay frowning with his face all screwed up. At least he was on my side.

"Right. Listen up as I call out who the top eight raffle ticket holders are this week. I must say it was very close, very close indeed. There were five other people who just missed out by one raffle ticket." There were lots of gasps and sighing around the mat as everyone looked around, wondering if they were the lucky ones, or the ones who had missed out.

"And I must say," Mr Higginbottom continued, "the introduction of the bonus tickets made all the difference. Some students wouldn't have made it otherwise. So do you really want to know, or do you want to wait until tomorrow?"

"Yes," we all called.

"Really, you don't sound too convincing," he teased.

"YEEEEEEEESSS!" we yelled, getting impatient but laughing at him at the same time. He was so funny.

"Alright, alright, you don't have to yell," he snorted. "So, in no particular order, the names are……Oh dear," he said. "I can't seem to read my writing. We'll have to boycott the competition. Who knows what boycott means?" There was no response, just more agitated murmurs as Mr H delayed the announcement.

"Come on, someone give it a try." Peter put up his hand. Goodness knows what he would say.

92

"Boycott means when boys hop in a cot," Peter laughed.

"No Peter," Mr H said slowly. "It means we will have to cancel the competition."

"NOOOOOOOOO!" half the class roared; the male half. The other half just sniggered until Mr H said, "Oh ok, I'll have a harder look at my list." He took a deep breath. "Right, enough mucking around. The first name is……. Sensational Sam, second is Nice Nigel," (*Nice!!!! What planet was Mr H on?*). "Next is, Jolly Joshua, Awesome Ali and Jiving Jacob, then electrifying Elly."

OH MAN!! *There it is*, I thought. She got in, *and* he called her electrifying. Far out. I wanted to die. I didn't want to go to school anymore. He continued with the names as I stewed on the fact that the untrustworthy new girl got in, and my name still hadn't been called. Finally the last two names were announced, and we were put out of our misery.

"Mad Matthew and finally, Rugged Rino,"

What was with all the adjectives? And what was with calling Nigel nice? More like, nasty, nosy, nit-picking Nigel, or even nasty, nose picking Nigel would probably have been more appropriate. But I didn't care. I was in, and Matthew was in after he picked up a few extra tickets from brown nosing the teacher. He wouldn't tell me what he did to get them though. Probably picked rotten sandwiches out of a mouldy trash can. But who cared? We were all in.

We grabbed our lunch as all the other boys left the room grumbling because they didn't get in. The girls were just rolling their eyes as they left, saying stuff like, "same old people that get in," or "boring, who cares?" I think they were all just jealous.

Sophie ran up to Elly and wished her good luck. She then went up to Mr Higginbottom as he was getting the equipment out.

"Mr H, can I keep Elly company since she's the only girl?"

"M'mmmm." He looked in deep thought for a moment. I guess he was thinking it over. "No can do, sorry Sophie. You know the rules. No spectators allowed. If I let you in, then I have to let every Tom, Dick and Harry in, and the computer room just isn't big enough. We'd end up looking like a smelly can of sardines. Maybe in the grand final, if she gets in." Well *that* wasn't going to happen; not in my lifetime anyway.

Sophie screwed her nose up in a pout and looked around for Elly, but Elly had disappeared. She was always disappearing before lunch. Weird!

We all raced into the computer room, grabbed a bean bag each and waited until Mr H booted up the consoles. I jumped in the Simpson's bean bag with the split in Homer's fly so I could see him peeing the little white balls out. It was about time the school repaired it, but it was so funny to watch.

We started munching quickly on our lunches as the consoles warmed up.

"Where are the games Mr H?" Matthew eagerly enquired.

"Hold your horses Mattie, we have to wait until everyone is here, and we're still missing one." Matthew looked puzzled.

"I don't have any horses sir," he said. I couldn't tell if he was joking or really believed Mr Higginbottom.

"Ah it's an expression, Matthew. It means HANG ON and be patient," Mr H yelled jokingly.

"Well where is she?" Jacob said, looking around. "She's the only one not here."

"Yeah, typical girl," I said, annoyed that she was causing trouble already.

"Can't you just tell us what games you've got?" asked Josh.

"Can we play Skylanders?" I love that game," said Ali getting hopeful.

"No Ali, sorry you can't choose the game. This time is going to be different. You are all going to compete on the same game, for the whole three heats." My eyes widened as I thought about it.

"Could be interesting," said Jacob, as Elly finally walked in with her lunch box. *Now she was going to hold us up eating her lunch.* "Come on Elly," Jacob urged. "Leave your lunch until later. We've eaten ours."

"Yeah good idea," said Matthew.

"Yeah hurry up," urged Sam.

"Leave her alone," Nigel piped in, as Elly started to look worried.

"Ooo sticking up for your girlfriend Nige," Sam fired back. "Lovers," he said in a teasing voice.

"GROW UP Sam," Josh butted in.

"Sorry Elly, but can't you just leave your lunch until after, so we can start?" Sam asked in a more pleasant voice. "We don't have much time."

"No I have to have my lunch. I'm sorry I took so long, but I've really got to eat," she replied.

"But can't you…."

"Shut it!" Nigel ordered. "She *has* to eat." He looked around at Elly as she quickly unwrapped her sandwich and shovelled it into her mouth. I actually felt a bit embarrassed that we'd tried to stop her from eating. It really wasn't a nice thing to do, even if she did seem a bit conniving herself. She was being so nice, it just didn't seem for real.

Sam grumbled under his breath, "Girls are such losers," but it was loud enough for me to hear.

"Yeah," I agreed softly, as I didn't want anyone else to hear me say it. Finally, someone was thinking straight. I didn't know what was up Nigel's nose, always sticking up for the new girl. Normally he hated girls. He was like president of the girl hater committee usually, especially girls that looked a little different like Elly. She didn't wear the latest fashions, her hair wasn't glued down with hairspray or pretty bits poking out of pony tails. She didn't hang around talking with the other girls all the time about useless stuff like makeup and instabam or whatever it is they talk about. She was definitely different.

My mom said that maybe she was a bit of a tom boy, because she liked to hang around with the boys and play soccer and stuff.

Sophie always tagged along with her like a faithful puppy dog though. She'd made at least one 'girl' friend.

"Ok, gather round my awesomely cool gamer super dudes......... oh and dudesses. Let's get the action started before we run out of time," Mr Higginbottom announced. "The rules are ..." He rambled them off so quickly in one of his funny voices that we could hardly understand. "No arguing. No cheating. No fighting, no whinging, and when you're out, you're out. Anyone that carries on like a pork chop sizzling on a bbq if they lose, will be picking up dirty bits of rubbish for a week, then cleaning all the bins.....with their tongue."

OH GROSS OUT BIG TIME! The others all looked around at each other with their eyebrows screwed up in knots all over their faces at the rank thought. Mr H is so funny, but sometimes he just gets a bit carried away with his own grossness.

"Right, time to unveil the notorious game that may be your weapon of destruction or your ultimate means to a destiny of greatness." I didn't know why he'd chosen to keep the game a secret for so long. There were only so many PS 3 games on this Earth. It couldn't have been *that* fantastic. Maybe he was finally going to allow us to play 'Grand Theft Auto' at school. Yeah right! Like that was never going to happen.

Finally, he pulled out four copies of a game I'd never seen before. It had this awesome picture of a dinosaur with its head exploding on it though.

"Coooooool!" Nigel exclaimed. "That looks sick as. I'm gonna dominate!" I squirmed at the sound of Nigel's gloating. I looked over at Josh to get his reaction but I was distracted when I noticed Elly's eyes light up when she saw the game. "Awesome," she said to Josh, who was sharing his bean bag with her. YUK. GROSS! SPEW! VOMIT. POO. What was he thinking? If he wasn't careful, he might get girl cooties. Girl germs are like 'everywhere' round this place. And germs are just like girls. They sneak and creep up on us, just like Elly. I think she was being a bit sneaky storming her way into the PS Club, pretending that she was being nice, but I knew she was up to something devious. No girl is ever that nice.

"My genius brother, has done something only the coolest, most awesome people can ever do. Can you believe, he has invented a PlayStation 3 game? And you lucky gamers get to be the first kids in the world ever to try it, before it is unleashed on the public. May I present, 'GALACTIC ZOMBIE'. Think yourselves highly privileged. Now, who shall verse who? That is the question."

I crossed my fingers and toes as Mr Higginbottom prepared to organise the heats. If I was against her, I would just die. This was one of those times when I needed to quickly pray and apologise to God for not praying very often. I began in my head looking upwards, because I think that's where he lives; up in the sky somewhere.

"Dear God, I know I don't pray much. Sorry about that. But this is one of those times when I really need your help. It's like, a real emergency. Please don't pair me up with Elly. Thankyou. I promise to do the dishes more regularly now, and I won't steal cookies out of Mom's secret stash."

"I've been wondering how to pair you up for the heats," Mr Higginbottom's words broke my religious concentration as he pulled a squashed, black magicians hat out of his brief case, and stuck his

head in upside down, pretending he was looking for something. When he surfaced out of the hat, he had a crumpled up, brightly colored handkerchief stuck in his left nostril.

"Oh that's where I left it," he laughed, pleased with himself. And then, as he pulled the hat away from his face, the handkerchief kept coming and coming in all shades of bright colors. Everyone started laughing madly, especially Matthew who was engrossed because he loves doing magic tricks.

"Ok, I have all your names in there on pieces of paper. Hopefully there are no goobers on them from this nasty hankie," he chuckled. "Right Rino and Elly, up here pronto. Winner of the first inaugural PlayStation playoffs versus the new kid on the block. Up here front and centre."

My heart plummeted to the ground as did my soul, my spirit, my whole life-force, my excitement, my energy and anything that existed happily in my body. Not *me* versus *her*. *Please no God! You promised.*

"AGHHHHHHHHHHHHHHHHHHHHHHHHHHHHHHHHHHHH
HHHHHHHHHHHHHHHHHHHH !!!!!!!!!!!!!!!!!!!!!!!!$$$$%%%!!!
################&&&&&&&&&&&&&****&&&&&%%
%%$#@@@@$%&&&******((()))))%%%%%%%%%@@@@@
@@@@####&&&71!!!!!@@@@@%$#@@##$%%%%%%%$$##@
@#$%%$#@@%^&*&^%$#@#$%%^^&&&&&&&&%%%%%%!!
&&&&&%%%%$#@@@@$%&&&******((()))))%%%%%%&&&
&&%%%%%$#@@@@$%&&&******((()))))%%%%%%&&&&&%
%%%$#@@@@$%&&&******((()))))%%%%%!!!!!!!!!!!!!!!!!!!"

100

22. Let the Games Begin

Elly jumped quickly out of the bean bag smiling brightly but I knew it was all fake. I got up reluctantly, not wanting to upset Mr Higginbottom, but I walked with my head held low, hiding the sulkiness rising in my face.

I so badly didn't want to verse Elly, and yet here it was happening to me. What had I done to deserve this cruel fate? It might be a boring match, but at least I could smash her, and she would be out of the competition and the PS Club once and for all, hopefully not wanting to return after her disgraceful loss to me.

"Ok, put your arms out in front of each other," Mr H commanded. I looked at him confused. "Come on, we haven't got all day. Scissors, paper, rock to see who puts their hand in the hat first to draw out a name." My heart soared through my body, escaped through my ear canal and rocketed through the universe doing a lap of the solar system, before it zoomed back into my body with renewed enthusiasm. Relief flooded every atom in my body as I realised I only had to verse Elly in 'scissors, paper, rock', not the real game.

She won and put her hand in the hat to draw out a name. I secretly hoped it would be Nigel so he could blitz her out, but she drew out Sam's name, much to his disgust. He looked at me and rolled his eyes. "Not a girl," he moaned. "Not fair!" Elly just laughed at his reaction, which was actually sort of cool, because most of the other girls usually get all offended and upset whenever we teased them, or they try and bite back with some stupid comment.

"Righto Rino, pick someone else to do scissors, paper, rock with."

I chose Josh and he beat me as well. He dug his hand in and pulled Ali's name out to play. Next I chose Matthew and he won too. I was on a loser's roll, which was a bit scary.

Mattie put his hand in the hat and drew out a rabbit. Mr Higginbottom shook his head laughing with the rest of us. "I knew there would be one clown who would find Petey way down there, and of course it had to be you Mattie." He ruffled Matthew's hair as he spoke, and then he kissed Petey the rabbit. Matthew put his hand in again and picked out Nigel's name which left me to verse Jacob. I was pretty pleased I didn't have to verse Matthew. I didn't want to put him out straight away. We all dashed over to the TV's which had warmed up and got into our positions.

"Everyone knows the rules. Let the games begin. You know the etiquette boys, ahhh and girl, I should say. Shake hands and give the pledge." We laughed at Mr Higginbottom's nonsense. The only pledge we ever said was, "Game on boys!" Another reason why girls should not be allowed in the club. It just didn't sound cool saying "Game on boys and girls." In fact, it sounded downright sissy. Oh man!

23. Galactic Zombie

We all paired up with our enemies, grabbed the bean bags and slid them into warfare territory to begin. It was going to be so hard playing a game that we were unfamiliar with, but we all had enough gaming history to be able to get the hang of it really quickly. We'd played enough zombie games, shapeshifter games, outer space games, war games, intergalactic games, action games, building games, crafting games. We'd done it all. This was just another one in a different setting.

Before the game started we got to create our avatars in a world set in the year 3000 in outer space called Tethysia where civilization had ceased to exist. The city had been blown up by shape shifting zombies that changed into creepy dinosaur-like, lizard men. They were downright butt ugly and **SCARY** with a capital S.

Jacob wanted to be the zombie which was fine by me. I created my character of a futuristic soldier with spiderman powers and supersonic eyes that could spit radiation beams of fire with one glance at the enemy. COOL! I called myself, Fire Lasher. Jacob called his avatar Zeek Serishia which had something to do with dinosaurs I think.

The aim of the game was to rebuild civilization and the city of Tethysia so it could become a thriving metropolis again, without getting killed by the zombies.

To begin, I had to create an army by spawning little creatures that roamed around called elfions. They were terrified and it took a while to find them as they were hiding in the ruins. I had to find slithers of gold from the walls of the sacred temple and reward them. Each slither was worth ten points and made the elfions transform into soldiers.

I trekked around the destruction site, smoke billowing around me from the rubble, looking for gold and creating soldiers. I had made four soldiers when the zombies started their attack on me. Every zombie had fifty lives, and when they killed an elfion they shapeshifted into the lizard man and got an extra life.

I pounded my supersonic radiation fire stream at the zombie and it let out a high pitched scream.

One life down. Only forty-nine to go. I fired the spider slime at him which was worth two lives and got him.

Forty-seven to go. POW! POW! POW ! Forty-four to go. This was easy peasy.

Then the zombie cackled in a curdling sound and threw a grenade at one of the elfions blowing it into smithereens, giving it back a life. It immediately changed into a lizard man, then ate another two of the elfions and spat their bones out, before chasing me with its tongue spitting in and out as I fired radiation fire beams at it, knocking off lives quickly.

I had to find a way to build shelter to protect myself from the zombies. Finally I found some bricks and was able to construct a house with sacred iron while the zombie was roaming around shooting pigions which were little creatures that gained them extra points.

"LOOK OUT," called Mr H as he saw the zombie try and attack the house. But I had enough of the sacred iron that I'd found to give the house immunity. From there I was able to create other buildings and find other elfions to build an army that outnumbered the zombies.

The game was so action packed and so lightning quick. I had to be thinking the whole time, creating and planning strategically to build the city, as well as dodge bombs and grenades. Every building I constructed gave me fifty points, but every building the zombies detonated gave them 100 points. It seemed so unfair and I was afraid I'd chosen the wrong character, because Jacob was leading 750 to 650 with only a few minutes left to go. It looked like this was going to be the first time in history that Jacob beat me?

NOOOOOOOOOOOOOOOO!

24. My Life in a Box

The game was seriously sick as, but it was also seriously hard; one of the hardest games I'd ever played. No amount of past experience in other games helped me, at all. I was crash burning badly, but I was an awesome gamer and my awesomeness didn't fail me. I won in the final minute of the game. I was definitely going to have to dig out my PS 3 on the weekend so I could practice, that was for sure. Mr H said he would let us borrow the game.

I couldn't believe Mattie and Josh both lost and were out. At least they didn't get put out by a girl, unlike Sam, who should have been ashamed of himself. If I was any younger, I would have taunted him with the childish chant, "beaten by a girl, beaten by a girl." But I was way too mature for that silly stuff. We just laughed at him, and poked him jokingly.

When I got home that afternoon, the house was a mess with junk all over the place and price labels everywhere. Even the dogs had labels stuck all over them. I figured Lisa must have got home before me, and she and Mom were into their yard sale stuff.

"So what I can I sell from your stuff?" Lisa asked me.

108

"You!" I replied.

"What?"

"You can sell *you*. In fact
I'm happy to *pay* someone to take
you away," I laughed jokingly.
Gee I could be a mean brother.
Funny, but mean.

"MOOOOOOOM!" Lisa shrieked. *Here she goes* I thought.
"Ryan's being mean already and he's only just walked in the door."

"Aw take a joke will ya," I said as I threw my bag on the bench.

"Take your bag off the bench please," Mom ordered as she
walked in carrying some old toys. I don't know why Mom worries
about the bench so much. What's the point of having a bench if we
can't put stuff on it?

I looked at the bundle of toys Mom had under her arm,
scrutinizing them for any that she might be trying to get rid of
illegally, without my permission. Mom does that sort of thing. There's
been heaps of times when I've spent the day looking for something
worth fifty dollars, only to find out Mom kindly donated it to the
Salvos for some kid to buy for twenty-five cents.

She had my old Buzz light year with one wing, under one arm,
Woody and Bullseye under her other arm and a ton of other injured
and legless superheroes under her chin. I had a pang of sadness saying
good-bye to those guys. It sort of reminded me of the Toy Story
movie when Woody gets upset when his owner gets rid of him.

"Mom! You can't get rid of the Toy Story stuff," I pleaded, and then I noticed my old dinosaurs. "Mom you can't throw those out. I still play with them."

"When was the last time you played with them?" she laughed. She got me there. I couldn't remember. It was probably like when I was four.

"But they're educational," and then I noticed my Tonka truck in a box with some other smashed up battery operated stunt cars without wheels. I pointed as I started to exclaim.

"Don't even go there," Mom said sternly. "They're broken, and they're going in the trash!" I felt a squirm of panic in my stomach seeing all my stuff go. I knew most of it was junk I hadn't played with, let alone *seen* in

years, but it was still heartbreaking to say my good byes. I gave Buzz Lightyear a kiss goodbye when Lisa wasn't looking, before Mom threw it in the box marked 'maybe'.

"What does 'maybe' mean Mom?"

"*Maybe* for the yard sale, *maybe* to the trash," she replied. Poor Buzz. He wasn't even good enough to be recycled to another kid. I wondered what Woody was thinking right now.

As I looked around, I saw another box marked MAYBE 2. And to my complete horror, my Minecraft figurines were lying helpless in that box, probably exhausted from attempting an escape up the cardboard walls. There was Steve, my cow and an enderman, all looking lost and forlorn among Lisa's barbie dolls. What complete torture for them – to be banished to the deathly dungeons of a barbie nether world.

"What the…?" I screamed. "Who put those in there? Where's Lisa?" Lisa came out from the pantry with a cookie crumbling in her gob just as I spoke. "YOU!" I pointed an accusatory finger at her as she entered the room. "I bet it was you."

"What?" She looked at me blankly. "What are you on about this time?"

"My Minecraft figurines. You stole them!" I had saved up and used some of my birthday money for those.

"What! You still play with dolls, at your age?" she taunted.

"THEY ARE NOT DOLLS. THEY ARE FIGURINES," I blasted, "and they cost me heaps, and they're new."

"Well they don't look new, and you said I could have anything in the garage, as long as I didn't take anything out of the bedroom." I remembered my words, and I remembered the other night when I was playing with the Minecraft figurines out in the garage.

"Someone forgot to put their toys away did they?" Mom chimed.

After rescuing my figurines, I grabbed a snack and raced upstairs to my bedroom. Friday afternoon was computer time. Two hours of uninterrupted, pure action time without any disturbances. YES!!!! I looked in my cupboard for my PS 3. I needed to practice Galactic Zombie. It wasn't going to be easy to win if I didn't practice, and I knew Nigel and Ali both had PlayStation 3's, so they would be practicing hard. The new girl Elly had said she didn't have one so she would be a push over. Maybe just for the next heat I wouldn't mind versing her, so I could win easy and get to the final.

I starting looking for the PS3 console, but decided to have a quick go of Minecraft online with Matthew and Josh. I loved Fridays. No homework and heaps of computer time without Mom nagging me all the time.

We played Skywars for what seemed like for ever. During the game I managed to get myself an iron sword from the centre chest. Awesome! But I won't say how many people I slayed with it.

I looked at the clock. It had been two hours that we'd been playing. I hadn't even thought of anything else, even food, except for searching for diamonds and slaying off mobs. Mom hadn't even called me down. She must have been in a good mood. Either that, or I didn't hear her because I had head phones on.

I thought I'd better try and dig out my old PlayStation 3 so I could start practicing. There was no way I would stand a chance beating Nigel if I didn't practice. I opened my toy cupboard to take a look inside, but it was pretty scary.

Misplaced bits of Lego and Bionicle pieces came gushing out at me like a rocky landslide set loose in motion. Spitfire, one of my Skylanders figurines came blasting off the top, before I quickly slammed the door shut again to stop the overflow. I had been looking for him for ages. My cupboard definitely needed a bit of a clean-up. But it would have to wait until next year when I had more time. I was too busy this year with all Mr Higginbottom's competitions.

I went to the other end of the cupboard and opened the larger door cautiously to see if anything else was going to come flying out at me like a projectile vomit. It was safe. I could see the box to my PlayStation 3 up high in the far end of the cupboard. I'm not supposed to climb the furniture. It's one of Mom's dumb rules, but this was an emergency, so I carefully started to climb the shelves finding a space between the crushed up boxes and toys for my oversized feet.

I had just about reached the box, when the shelf below me suddenly made a large cracking sound, breaking into shards and taking me with it. My head and chin ricocheted off the highest shelf and as I spiralled towards the ground in a flurry, I kept thinking that I wouldn't be able to play soccer the next morning, because I would be dead.

25. Dead or Alive

Mom came running up the stairs at the sound of the crashing. I realized I was still alive so I began to panic that I was going to get into trouble.

"Are you alright?" I heard her call as she came up the stairs. Maybe if I shouted back that my head was hanging off my neck and blood was spurting everywhere and my right leg wasn't attached to my hip anymore, she might be relieved and go lightly on me when she realized I was ok.

"What on earth were you doing?" she said with a frown, when she witnessed my catastrophe as I lay on the ground surrounded by all my plastic friends. Action man had landed on my face and a whole bucket of Lego landed on top of my private parts. At least it wasn't my Dead Pool with his swords. That would be a bit painful.

"Are you alright?" Mom asked, her motherly instincts kicking in."

"Yes, I think so."

"No blood?"

"No, I don't think so."

"Anything broken?"

"No I don't think so."

"Well get up and clean up this mess, and maybe now you'll realise why I say DO NOT CLIMB ON THE FURNITURE!" And with those unloving, unsympathetic words, Mom stormed off down the stairs. I bet if it was Lisa who fell, Mom would be all lovey-dovey, hugging her and administering first aid and checking her over. She'd probably even go and get some candy from her secret stash to make it all better. It's so unfair around this place sometimes.

As I started to pick off the bits of Lego from my private region, I heard Mom come back up the stairs in a hurry, huffing and puffing. "And as soon as you've finished, come down and have your supper, and then straight to bed. You've got an early soccer match in the morning."

"But Mom…." I cried out.

"No buts, just do it," she answered back abruptly. I wondered if she would have been this angry if she'd come up and found me with two broken legs and gashes across my face, or worse still, if she'd found me dead. Probably.

26. Good Morning, NOT

The next morning I was having an insane dream about a Minecraft city that I was building. It was one of those crazy Minecraft dreams that I have regularly (like, every night).

Everywhere I went, I was able to tame wolfs with bones, but zombies and Endermen were everywhere, fighting the zombies from Galactic Zombie. It was probably because I had been in such a deep sleep because the night before I had been kept awake all night by Mom and Lisa doing their yard sale setup. I think they were still labelling toys at midnight.

I'd just fired a TNT ignited arrow through one of the zombies when I heard a loud banging noise penetrating my sleep. The rapping was soft at first but got louder until I was full on awake.

I looked over to my Thomas the Tank clock, and I thought it said 5 am. It must have been 8 am, but it still seemed dark. I looked again. 5 am. 5 AM!!!!!!!!!!! What? What was that banging at five am? Was I still dreaming?

I looked out my bedroom window. It wasn't light yet but the beginnings of a new day sparkled gently onto the street giving enough visibility to show three cars parked out the front of our house and a group of people at our front door knocking. So much for Lisa's sign that said 'strictly 8am-12pm'.

I got back into bed and tried to get back to sleep but it was useless. I tossed and turned, and smothered my head with the pillow but I still couldn't sleep.

By 6 am Dad had started to let people into the garage and the front yard selling them stuff. I spied from my bedroom window. I didn't want to go down because some of them looked like real weirdos, including weirdo beardo, the screwball from down the street.

Some people pulled up in vans, some had trailers, and some came on bikes with backpacks. The things they bought were ridiculous. I was really happy Dad and I had to leave for soccer at 7am, even though I was a bit stiff and sore from my fall the night before.

I put on my uniform and ambled into the hall. Lisa was in the bathroom, like she always is when I'm busting to pee. And when I'm busting for number two she always seems to take even longer. I swear she knows when I need to do a poo and she locks herself in the bathroom.

"Hurry will ya," I called out, as I rapped on the door.

"I've just got in here, and I need to have a shower."

"You have to go down and help in your yard sale. Dad has to take me to soccer now." I rapped on the door louder, as I spoke.

"GO AWAY," came the reply.

"Hurry up, I'm busting."

"You're always busting when I'm in here."

"That's because you're always in there," I shouted, getting angrier as the tingling feeling in my willy threatened to bust out.

"Well I have to have a shower and then do my make up, and then.."

"You don't need to have a shower, just go down and help. No-one's going to care if you stink or look ugly. They just want to buy stuff."

"What would you know? What if there's a cute boy come to buy stuff and I look like a swamp monster?"

"Well you will, no matter how long you stay in there," I said, under my breath as I ran down stairs to the spare toilet.

Ahhhhhh relief, finally.

I had my breakfast and Dad and I finally took off to soccer leaving Mom and a mob of frenzied people looking for the next biggest bargain this side of the universe. I hoped by the time we got back it would be nearly over, and the hordes of cheapskate bargain hunters were back in their own yards.

27. The Case of the Missing PS3

As we drove back home, I hoped and prayed that all the looneys had left our yard, and Mom and Lisa had sold everything so there was no cleaning up to do.

As we rounded the corner coming into our street I spotted someone walking along who I really didn't want to see. I quickly ducked down into the seat but I think it was too late. I think she saw me, which probably made it look really weird.

"Who was that?" Dad asked.

"Who was what?" I replied.

"That girl you just saw and ducked down from."

"I didn't see any girl, I just……..I just ..ah.. was looking for money…in the seat here." Dad laughed at me.

"Well she must have seen *you* because she just waved as you ducked down to find your money. Is she your girlfriend?"

"WHAT? DAAAAD! NO! GOD NO. Puke stuff. Vomit. No way is *she* my girlfriend." I could feel my cheeks blushing. "No way is *anyone* my girlfriend. Why would you think that Dad?"

"Oh, but I thought you didn't see anybody," Dad said, sneaking in a sly smile.

"OK! She's the enemy. She's a new girl and she's probably stalking me to try and find out my game plan for the competition next week, and then sabotage it." Dad looked puzzled. His nose and eyebrows crumpled up, nearly meeting each other in the middle.

"How on earth would she sabotage your game by walking innocently down the street carrying a bag?"

"What? She was carrying a bag?" I eyed my dad suspiciously.

"People are allowed to carry bags Rino."

"Yeah, but what's she doing down this way? Weird. She's weird Dad. Can we just leave it?"

When we got back to the house, there were still a few people mingling around. Lisa was like a hyper bunny on double strength batteries jumping all over the place.

"I've made so much money. I'm in the money, I'm in the money," she sang.

"Well remember you have to give me my cut for my things," I reminded her.

"Yeah yeah," she replied in a droll tone.

"How can I trust you, that you'll give me the right money?"

"Oh grow up. I'm not dishonest like you. I'll give you the money when I count it all out at the end of the day."

I raced inside and left Mom, Dad and Lisa to the last of their bargain-hunting guests. I had some serious home work to do. I needed to find my PlayStation 3 and get practicing the game if I was going to stand a chance at winning.

I trepidly opened my cupboard with the broken shelf and had a good look around without letting anything escape. The box was there, but it was empty. I had a look under the bed. I laughed when I remembered how I used to be scared of monsters under the bed when I was five. Alright, when I was six, ok maybe seven, or eight, but definitely not now. Now I know there's no monsters under the bed, because monsters don't exist anywhere, except in the bedroom next door, and there's only one of her.

It was starting to drive me batty not being able to find the PlayStation 3, when I finally remembered a few months ago I needed the box to make a house for a lizard, so I took the PlayStation out into the garage, and left it sitting on one of Dad's shelves. It also reminded me that I forgot to clean the box after the lizard escaped and it was sitting in my cupboard with old bits of lizard poo and wee, mixed with dried up grass in it. YUK! I thought I better chuck it out as soon as I found the PlayStation.

I went down stairs into the garage and straight to the spot where I'd left the PS 3. Not there! I hunted all around the garage which was a complete mess because of the yard sale. Nowhere to be found, and it was even more of a mess after I'd finished looking.

I started to panic, then a massive brain wave came over me. Dad had probably put it back into the sewing room. Even though Mom said she was going to start sewing things, she never did, so the room doubled as a junk room. If there wasn't a place for something, it went straight to the junk room. That's where it would be.

I opened the door, and was greeted by a scene not unlike my overflowing cupboard. There was stuff everywhere, on the floor, on the sofa, the window sill, the sewing table. The cupboard wasn't closed properly because there was stuff cascading out everywhere. But it didn't matter. I had to find the PS3.

After half an hour of turning the junk room upside down, I started to panic. Worse than panic! I started to hyperventilate in fear. My mouth started to froth at the corners and steam started to billow out of my head, and my heart started to push through the walls of my chest as it raced a million miles per hour. Ok I might be exaggerating a little bit. But I was afraid. I was scared. What if I couldn't find my PS 3? How could I practice the game? How could I beat Nigel?

I ran out to the front yard to find Mom and Dad cleaning up.

"Oh how nice you've come out to help us clean up," Dad said smiling.

"Dad where's my PlayStation?"

"Underneath the TV cabinet where it always is."

"NO! Not my PS4, my PS 3."

"Good grief, you have far too many PlayStations son. I don't know where it is."

"It's in the garage," Mom interjected.

"Where in the garage Mom?" I said, starting to feel a little bit more relieved.

"Up on Dad's book shelf."

"Noooo. I looked there. That's where it used to be. But it's not there now."

"Oh well, it was there a couple of days ago. I remember seeing it there when I was sorting stuff out for the yard sale."

"Oh NO! You sold it in the yard sale didn't you?"

"Don't be silly Rino. Of course we didn't," Mom replied laughing.

"Dad. Did you sell it?"

"I was at soccer with you remember? The only thing I sold was a dirty feather duster that someone bought for free when I got back."

"Well, what about Lisa? Where's Lisa? She might have sold it."

"Don't be silly Ryan. Lisa wouldn't sell your PlayStation," Mom said.

"Oh yeah, wanna bet?" That would be just the sort of thing Lisa would do. "Where is she anyway?"

"She's gone out with one of her friends to spend some of her money," Mom remarked.

"Probably *my* money," I replied under my breath.

It was pretty typical of Lisa to escape as soon as the cleaning up began. Mom continued with her 'stick up for Lisa' moment.

"Ryan, she sold mostly *her* stuff and she's saved the money for you for your stuff. And I was here all the time except for when I went to the bathroom, and she didn't sell your PlayStation. I think I'd notice. She didn't even give it away," Mom added. I face palmed myself in despair at the thought of Lisa wrapping up my PS3 and giving it away to some stupid five year old.

"Rino, get a grip of yourself. You look like a guppy fish about to be attacked by a shark. And anyway, would it be such a really bad thing, if you did actually give your PS3 away to some unfortunate child who doesn't have a loving rich family to buy him or her things? Would it really be the end of the world?"

I thought about Mom's words and realised that once again, she was right. I had a PS4, way better than a PS3, with awesome games. I'd had three awesome years playing my PS3 before moving on to the PS4. It probably would be a really nice idea if I could give it to someone that was poor. Except for the fact that Galactic Zombie could only be practiced on a PS3. So that poor kid, whoever he was, wasn't going to get a free PS3 from me anytime soon. That's if I could even find it.

WHICH WAS NOT HAPPENING IN A HURRY!!

28. The Suspect Files

I ran back to the garage and checked the spot where it was supposed to be again, and again and again. I checked everywhere. I turned the whole house completely upside down. The only spot I hadn't looked was Lisa's bedroom. I didn't think it would be in there, and I really didn't want to venture in to that scary place. There were weird things in that room, like bras and undies lying all over the place, and make up, like everywhere. Then she has this row of eerie looking china dolls sitting on a shelf with a creepy looking clown in the middle. One of them even has an eye poked out and she won't get it fixed or throw it out. They all just stare (even one-eyed Isabelle) eerily at the door, waiting; waiting for somebody. I **HATE** walking into her room at night with those eyes glaring at me.

I decided there was no point in looking in her room. There was no way Lisa would put it in there. She would know she would be sprung if she was going to hide it there. I thought of the possibility that she had taken up gaming herself, but then I threw that thought on the dump pile along with all the other thoughts I have about her.

There's no way she would play cool games. It might take up her instabam time or her Backchat stuff.

I was just about to throw myself on the bed and have a tantrum (an inner tantrum where no-one hears me) when the phone rang. It was Mattie. He'd left his soccer boots in my dad's car. He's always leaving stuff behind everywhere. His dad says it's because he always leaves his brain in bed sleeping while he goes off somewhere. I think Matthew gets his silly humor from his dad.

I told him about the case of the missing PlayStation. He was horrified, because he knew how important practicing for the competition on a PlayStation3 was.

"Maybe someone has set you up and they've stolen it so you can't practice?"

"What! Really? You think someone would do that?"

"Stranger things have happened," he said in an eerie voice with sound effects like he was in a horror movie.

"Matthew don't make that sound."

"Scaredy cat!"

"I'm not. It's just weird. You're weird," I laughed.

"Do you want me to come over and help you look for it?" he asked.

"Nah, there's no point. It's not here. It's gone. You know what?"

"What? You're dumb and I'm not."

"No Matthew, it's the other way around actually. No I think you're right. Someone's stolen it, and I have to get to the bottom of it and find out who."

"And why?" he added.

"Why?" I asked.

"Why what?"

"What why?" We sounded like a ping pong match gone wrong.

"What? You're not making sense," Matthew added.

"And you are?" I defended.

"To me I am," Matthew answered, "but you sound like you're a nerd from outer space."

"I just mean, oh I don't know what I mean. I'm all confused now," I declared, frustrated up to my eyeballs. "I don't even know what I was saying."

"You have to find out 'why' someone has stolen your PS3. You have to find the motive, and when you find the motive you are one step closer to finding the killer, I mean the thief, red handed." This time he spoke like he was advertising a crime show.

I decided that if Mom had definitely seen the PlayStation a few days ago, it had to have been taken by someone. Our garage was always open. It would be easy for someone to sneak in quickly and take it. The position where it had been was in full view of anyone walking past.

"Who do you think it could be?" I asked Matthew.

"Josh!" he replied quickly.

"What! Are you karazeeeee?" I slammed. "He's my mate, and he's not even in the competition anymore. And he *has* a PlayStation 3."

"I know but it's the ones you think you know," he began slowly in a deep, husky voice, "they're the dangerous ones. You think they have it all. But deep down inside there's a time bomb ticking away just waiting to be detonated. And Josh's bomb was probably fuelled by jealousy when you got in the comp and he didn't. And he probably wants the new girl to win." Matthew then made a sound effect from the jaws movie when the shark is approaching. He is such a kook. "Now he's going to sabotage your chances."

"What the ....! What are you on Matthew? Can you hear yourself? Josh would NOT sabotage my chances. And even if for some strange reason, a psycho zombie took over him and he *did* want to ruin my life, his goody goody side would kick in and take over the zombie and prevent him from stealing anything. Hek, Josh wouldn't even steal a flower for his Mother from his neighbor's garden on Mother's Day last year."

"Yeah, you're right. Back to the drawing board. Oh I gotta go. We're going out for a picnic for Dad's birthday. Seeya."

"Ok Seeya, have fun at your teddy bear's picnic," I said sarcastically. "Seeya at school."

I decided I needed to take some serious action and get to the bottom of the stolen PS3. I was going to have to make a list; a list of possible suspects, possible motives, possible opportunities, possible witnesses and character profiles. I was going to find out 'who dunnit' if it killed me.

I would have to make **The Suspect Files.** I was going to smoosh me a baddie. I always fancied myself as a bit of a super hero detective but it never happened. Once I tried to become like Spiderman and I let a daddy long legs spider crawl all over me because I couldn't find one with a red stripe. But I didn't get spider powers, I just got very itchy.

Another time I tried to fly off the roof of the shed wearing mom's flowery apron pretending I was superman, but I didn't fly. I just got a lot of cuts and bruises.

The big problem of being a super hero, is you have to be fearless, and my big problem is that I'm always a bit of a chicken, scaredy cat, big woos, whatever you want to call it, in scary situations.

But now was my chance to be Super Rino and solve the case of the missing PS3 and slam the bad dude responsible by karate chopping his head off. Ok, maybe not.

While I thought about who would be on the suspect file list, I played Minecraft to help me concentrate. But the whole time I was playing, I couldn't help but think about why Matthew would say Josh would want the new girl to win. I kept thinking back to school when he was staring at her all the time. That really worried me. Oh no! I hope Josh wasn't starting to go all goo gaa on me.

Suspect No 1 Nasty Nige

Suspect no 2 Smelly Elly with the skinny belly.

Suspect no 3 Weirdo Beardo, screwball from up the street

Suspect no 4 Weirdo Beardo's brother

Suspect no 5 Loony Lisa.

SUSPECT 1

NAME: Nasty Nigel

MOTIVE : He's a bully, and mean, and jealous

OCCUPATION: Student, and part-time bully

DESCRIPTION: Glasses, nerdy, black spikey hair and boogers

PRIOR CRIMES: being mean all the time, stealing gum from me in 2nd grade

SUSPECT 2

NAME: Smelly Elly with the skinny belly

MOTIVE : Wants to win, hasn't got a PS3

OCCUPATION: student, and evil manipulator

DESCRIPTION: skinny, weird looking, curly fuzzy hair, Tom boy

PRIOR CRIMES: evilness (probably), assisting in bullying

SUSPECT 3

NAME: Weirdo Beardo from down the street

MOTIVE : he likes stealing, looks weird

OCCUPATION: Full time thief

DESCRIPTION: weird, scary, grey beard

PRIOR CRIMES: been in gaol (I think)

SUSPECT 4

NAME: Weirdo Beardo's brother

MOTIVE: He likes stealing, looks weird

OCCUPATION: Thief's assistant

DESCRIPTION: weird, scary, red beard with bits of old food in

PRIOR CRIMES: maybe he was in gaol too

SUSPECT 5

NAME: Loony Lisa

MOTIVE: She likes to annoy me

OCCUPATION: Annoying sister

DESCRIPTION: Annoying

PRIOR CRIMES: Being annoying

29. The Nigelly Conspiracy

During the week, I kept my eyes and ears to the ground trying to hear if there was any reason for anyone to become a suspect. I didn't directly ask anyone if they'd stolen my PS3, but I tried to secretly get a few answers by asking sly questions, but I came up with a big, fat nothing.

Finally, the week came to a close, and I managed to get a raffle ticket every day, but unfortunately so did Elly and Ali, and of course so did Nigel. They were all on their best behavior and doing all their class work really well. I'd never seen Nigel behave so perfectly. It was scary really. My suspicions grew monstrously that he and Elly were hatching some devious plan. They were pretending to be really smooth and well behaved, but deep down they were ready to attack.

I tried to tell Josh and Matthew what I thought about the Nigel and Elly conspiracy, but they just laughed at me. "It's the Nigelly conspiracy theory. You just watch it. They're working incognito in cahoots with each other, but they're going to take over at the last minute, and stamp all over us."

Josh replied shaking his head, and laughing. "How can they work together? It's a PlayStation game that neither have played before. They might even end up versing each other."

"Yeah we'll see, won't we?" I replied suspiciously.

During the second week of the competition, I was getting desperate. There were only two days to go and my PlayStation still hadn't turned up anywhere. I had even posted a few notices on trees around my street saying missing PS3, reward given. I didn't know what reward I was going to give, but I was desperate. No–one rang the phone number anyway. The only person that mentioned it was Dad who saw it when he was taking the dogs for a walk, and I got into trouble because I put my address on the poster.

He said any Tom, Dick or Harry could come to our house now and steal stuff. And I replied that some Tom, Dick or Harry had already come to our place and stolen my PS3. They didn't need an invitation.

Josh offered to let me use his PS3 on the Wednesday night so I pretended we had a homework assignment and I went around to his house and played for two hours. It really helped. I got the gist of the game a lot more and felt I was a bit more prepared for any action on the Friday.

The Friday was finally getting close. I couldn't wait. Having to wait the fortnight instead of every week was pure agony. The school board put a real downer on the PlayStation club by changing the rules, but as Mom reminded me, we were very lucky to even get to play PlayStation at school. She told me we should just shut our mouths and be happy with what we had. I guess she was right. There was no other school that I knew of where you could play it. But then again, no other school had a teacher as awesome as Mr H.

Thursday lunch time came and we were all sitting on the mat waiting for Mr Higginbottom to see who got all the criteria for the day and who would get something out of the green bucket.

As usual, I knew I didn't have a worry as I'd worked like crazy all day to get good marks for everything.

He got out his big black book and looked at all the names.

"Not many names today because there was a bit of trouble at lunch time I hear." There were a few knowing groans around the class. Obviously some of the kids knew they were not going to get called out because of some food fight incident that happened at the cafeteria. Apparently some of the kids got carried away during morning break, and there were a few meat pies found squished on people's faces not to mention yoghurt dripping very charmingly from the head of a couple of boys. I wished I'd seen it. It would have been hysterical.

"Yes, a little disappointing," Mr H continued, "because I've been given a list of some boys from this grade that were involved in a certain incident at the cafeteria today. Yes that's right, 'BOYS'. No girls were involved. What does that say boys?" Mr Higginbottom questioned us disapprovingly.

"That the boys are more fun and more adventurous," Peter called out. Man he could be stupid sometimes.

"No Peter. That is not what it tells me."

Matthew whispered into my back. "The girls are more boring."

I giggled quietly. "Yeah and they're always on diets so they don't want to have food fights." Matthew tried to stifle a laugh but in doing so he let one go out the other end.

"MATTHEW!" The class chorused. Matthew's cheeks glowed. For someone who was the fart king of the school yard, he always got very embarrassed in close quarters on the class mat, but we all laughed hysterically. Mr Higginbotton wasn't impressed.

"Grade Five, I don't think this is a laughing matter. Matthew's manners may be under developed, but we have quite a few boys on this list here who obviously have even *less* manners. In fact I would go as far as saying, a pig in mud would have more manners than what you boys have demonstrated today in the cafeteria."

All the boys hung their heads; some in shame, some just because they didn't know where to look. We could see Mr Higginbottom wasn't impressed, and we hated disappointing him. "So I will continue, but there will be a few names not on the list that should have been here. First up, the criteria is,

One - spelling today 10 /10 and no less.

Two : Have read up to Chapter 5 in Deltora Quest.

Three : Book report handed in to me from your favorite novel. Anyone who did the report on a picture book will automatically fail.

Four : The maths fractions worksheet completed and handed in today. I still have three missing so those three people definitely don't meet the criteria today. And of course number five is that you haven't been in any trouble today from me or any of the other wonderful teachers at this school."

He continued, "so we have Sophie and we have Elly." I looked around to spy on Elly's reaction, but she looked like she wasn't listening. She was sort of lying back against one of the tables rolling her eyes around. She looked weird. I ignored her and kept listening as Mr H continued. "We have Jay, we have Josh, Cheryl, Ella, Matthew. Good to see *you* stayed out of trouble today Matthew." Matthew grinned proudly at Mr H's words. Thank goodness he didn't have lunch money that day. "And finally we have Ali and Sarah."

My heart stopped.

It skipped a beat.

It started racing.

It started catapulting.

It started bungee jumping all over the place zig zagging across the room in horror.

Was Mr H having a little joke with me? He must have been. I hadn't done anything wrong. Had I? I handed everything in. Didn't I? I got ten out of ten for spelling. I think. Yes I did. What was going down?

30. SUS! BIG TIME

The girls all took chocolate bars of course, except for Elly, who got a raffle ticket, and along with the boys, put it directly into the red bucket. As she got up, she tripped on the mat and stumbled to the ground. It was hilarious, but no one really laughed as she tried to regain her balance with great difficulty.

Even though Matthew and Josh were out of the competition, they were allowed to still come and watch, so they took a raffle ticket too. I started counting the number of tickets I'd put in, to see if I would still have enough to make the top eight. Nigel had got one every day, so had Elly and Ali, so they were safe.

I wondered whether I should wait until the next day to see if I still made it into the top eight, or whether I should say something to Mr Higginbottom straight away. As everyone started getting restless, and fidgeting, I watched Elly sneak off from the mat. She seemed to be acting a little weirdly. I saw Nigel get up and follow her, and while everyone was chatting amongst themselves, I saw them go up to Mr H's desk. That was really bizarre.

"How come you didn't get the criteria?" Matthew asked me.

"Ah….what?" I replied, trying to look past him to see why Elly was loitering around the desk. No-one was supposed to hang around the teacher's desk, but Mr Higginbottom was too busy to notice.

"You didn't make the criteria. How come?" Josh repeated.

"Hang on, I need to get a drink," and I jumped up and headed towards my desk walking past Elly and Nigel on purpose. I knew they were up to something and maybe it had something to do with me not getting a ticket.

"What's up his butt?" I heard Josh ask Matthew. But I wasn't interested in what they were saying because as I walked to my desk, I saw Nigel getting candy out of Mr H's desk and smuggling them to Elly. **Whoaaaa!**

Ok it may have only been candy, but it was stealing, and stealing is stealing no matter what it is. I didn't want to be a dobber or anything, but I thought it was pretty low of them just to go and steal from Mr Higginbottom, especially when he was in the room. I knew that Elly was a fake. So much for saying she never ate candy. LIAR! I wondered what else she had in store. Maybe she'd done something sly to stop my name getting in Mr H's black book.

I didn't know what to do. I wasn't going to snitch. That wasn't my thing. I went back to the mat just as Mr Higginbottom was dismissing us out to lunch. His last words were, "as part of the competition, I am now going to count the raffle tickets on Thursday at lunch time, so today was your last chance to get a raffle ticket before the big competition tomorrow. Good luck everyone, dismissed for lunch. Oh and I will be having a word later with those involved in the airborne food spectacular."

I skulked off. At least I didn't have to be worried about getting into trouble because of the food fight incident where someone apparently ended up with half a burrito stuck in their ear. Wish I'd seen it though!

As we sat having our lunch, Matthew ran up and tapped me on the shoulder. "Aren't you going to ask H'man why you didn't get a raffle ticket?"

"Nah. I'll still get in," I said, though secretly I was really worried, and obsessing over why I didn't get a raffle ticket. It was really bugging me.

"Go and ask him," suggested Josh.

"Nah! I'll get in!" I repeated, getting up to get my handball out of my bag. "What is she doing?" I said, as I noticed Elly slumped up against the wall, outside the classroom with her head between her knees. The way she was sitting, we could see her knickers. Gross out! "She is so weird that new girl," I said to the others.

"Why?"

"Why is she weird? Well look at her," I said, frowning as they stared at Elly rolling around on the ground. I started laughing but stopped instantly when Josh frowned at me.

"Don't laugh, that's cruel." Straight away I felt remorse. I knew Josh was right. It didn't matter how weird other kids were, you should never laugh at them. Maybe I just laughed because I felt uneasy.

"I knew she was different, but I didn't know she was so freaky. Hey you'll never guess what I saw her do before?"

"Quit it Ryan," commanded Josh staring intently at Elly. His look scared me. "Is she ok?" he said.

But before I could answer, Nigel came running from the opposite direction with a can of drink, knocking me out of the way, and shoved it into her mouth.

"Get out of the way," Nigel barked as he dribbled soda into her mouth. Maybe he stole that for her as well. He seemed to be her little run around slave. "Get Mr Higginbottom," he yelled at us.

Matthew and I looked at each other stunned, as Sophie ran out of the classroom with Mr Higginbottom's jar of jelly beans again, and Josh sprinted off towards the staffroom. I couldn't believe it. Was Sophie stealing lollies for her now as well? The whole scene was a total confusing chaos.

31. Greedy Candy Thief

Elly grabbed the jar and quickly put three of the colorful candy into her mouth greedily. She was still lying on the ground, but Nigel was holding her head up.

I'd only just started to realise that something was seriously wrong when Mr Higginbottom, Miss Egbutt and Miss Dorklands raced around the corner in a panic. Mr Higginbottom started speaking quickly to her and he seemed very relieved when she spoke back.

"I'm feeling ok now," she said. Nigel's quick thinking with his lemonade really helped me, and Sophie had to sneak into the classroom to get my jelly beans, I'm sorry."

"Oh don't be sorry," Miss Egbutt said. "That's what they're there for. Should we ring your mom?"

"I don't live with my mom. I only live with my dad. But it's ok. I'm used to it. This kind of thing happens every now and then."

I immediately felt a pang of regret when I heard her say something about *her* jelly beans. They were *her* jelly beans, not Mr Higginbottom's. I felt like I was gawping but the whole scene was kind of really weird, and I don't mean because Nigel was actually helping someone.

Josh had raced up to us, following the teachers, after he notified them of Elly's strange behavior.

"I think she's a diabetic," Josh whispered to me, looking across to the frantic scene. "I heard the teachers say something when I said they had to come quick to Elly."

"What's a diabetic?" asked Matthew.

"Der! Don't you know anything?" I whispered, teasing him, and trying to make out I wasn't staring at Elly.

"Not really," he chuckled. "What is it?"

"I don't know either," I laughed. "Isn't it, like, when you're allergic to peanuts or something?"

"Gee you guys are dumb," Josh interrupted quietly. But before he could inform us, Elly interrupted.

"It's ok guys. You don't have to whisper. It's not a freak show and I won't charge you 10 c. I'm a diabetic. No big deal," she smiled, a sense of normality rising in her face again.

I really felt quite guilty about the things I'd said, and the way I'd laughed when she was rolling on the floor showing her knickers. But I still didn't know what a diabetic was. I wondered whether I should ask her, but cheeky Matthew beat me to it.

"So what's a diabetic then? Are you allowed to eat peanuts?"

"Yes," she laughed. "Of course. I just have to be careful with the amount of sugar I have. My insulin doesn't work properly to help take the sugar from the blood into the cells. So I have to inject insulin

149

into my body to help it. Dad says the insulin is like a bus taking the sugar people to the cells where they need to go. Sometimes the insulin bus works too well and it takes too many sugar people away from my blood and I have a hypo, like just now, when there's not enough sugar in my blood stream. I can get all dizzy and confused, and sometimes even angry. But it's quickly fixed with candy and soda. That's one of the good things about being diabetic," she laughed again. She wasn't at all embarrassed or ashamed. "Even though I'm not allowed to eat candy normally, when I have a hypo, that's the quickest thing to fix it."

"So you have to give yourself needles?" Matthew asked.

"Sure do. Wanna see me do one tomorrow?"

"Ahhhh, noo thanks," Matthew replied quite firmly. "That's not on my list of cool things to do this year, sorry."

"Josh? Ryan? Any takers?" she asked laughing.

"Noooooo," we both said together, as we all chuckled.

"I will," volunteered Nigel.

"You've seen it before Nigel," Elly said.

"How come Nigel's seen it?" Matthew inquisitively asked.

"Because I live next door to him." Finally I realised why Elly was spending so much time with Nigel. She couldn't help it. He was her next door neighbor. Poor sucker. I didn't know who to feel more sorry for. She probably didn't have any friends when she moved here, so he was better than no-one.

"And Nige's been coming over a lot to practice the game on my PS3," she continued. I looked at Matthew, stunned. Was he thinking what I was thinking? His face was blank so I wasn't sure. I looked across to Josh but he was intent on asking Elly questions about diabetes. Josh wanted to be a doctor when he grew up.

She had a PlayStation 3!

She had a PlayStation 3!

Last week she didn't have one and I did. This week she had one and I didn't.

Something smelt fishier than a crate of sardines baking out on a hot road.

I think I'd found my thief.

32. The Top Eight

Before I got to interrogate the accused and cross-examine the witnesses, the school bell rang and we had to go back to class. Everything had returned to normal with Elly, and I soon forgot about her suspected criminal activity because Mr Higginbottom announced he had counted all the raffle tickets and he knew who the eight top ticket holders were that were going into the PS club on Friday.

I was pretty confident that I would still have enough tickets, even though I'd missed out on one, but my heart decided to play its crazy gremlin game anyway trying to escape out of my chest.

Mr H wouldn't tell us until the end of the day, which meant we had to sit through an afternoon of boring Maths and English before we found out. But for the last hour we went outside and got to play British Bulldog. Awesome.

I was absolutely gobsmacked. Usually when we play British Bulldog, the girls do nothing but squeal and carry on like barbie dolls. Actually they're more like monster high dolls. But Elly was unreal. She caught so many kids. She was faster than most of the boys, except for Josh and me. Ever since the substitute teacher made us run all the time, I had become a lot fitter and faster. Maybe next time when we had to pick teams I would pick Elly.

WHAT WAS I SAYING? There was no room for thieves on my team no matter how good they were.

As we all sat on the mat, exhausted, dripping with salty sweat and smelling of stinky socks and underarm b.o, Mr H got out his infamous black book and prepared to make the grand announcement.

"Right class, tomorrow, these eight people may be permitted entry to the awesome PS club whether you are in the final, or would just like to have a gawp. Here are the names." He paused as we all listened intently but he didn't continue. There was just a deadly silence as we grew impatient as Mr H kept looking down into his black book.

Then of all the weird things, Mr H started snoring. We all looked around puzzled and started laughing hysterically until he woke with a grunt and a gurgle and started again. I knew he was just being a big fake but I'm sure some of the girls believed him.

"Oh dear, see how tired you make me. Right let's see. Nigel, Ali, Matthew, Josh, Jacob, Rino, Elly. Peter and Jay." He rattled the names off quickly.

Phewwwwww! Despite missing out on one raffle ticket that day, I still made the top eight. I was definitely relieved. But it still annoyed me as to why I didn't get one. And it still plagued me as to whether Elly had stolen my PS3. I decided I would have to find out both mysteries.

33. Outthink Outsmart and Outplay

The next day I was really edgy. I'd hardly had any practice on the PS3 with the new game, but I knew Elly and Nigel had practiced heaps. I guessed Ali probably did as well. I would have to rely on my awesome gaming skills, my ability to devise strategy, my kick ass timing and quick thinking. I was going to have to use all those skills to out think, out smart and most of all, out play the enemy; whoever that lucky sucker was going to be.

As we had lunch quickly on the Friday before the competition, we chatted together excitedly.

"Who do you think you will verse today Rino?" asked Jacob.

"Hopefully Nigel. I'll kick his ass out, and then it will be easy in the final. The dosh will be all mine," I laughed.

"Yeah well, don't underestimate Ali. He's a pretty cool player, and I heard he's been practicing like, every day."

"Oh man. That's what I was afraid of. It's so unfair. They all have a PS3 except me." I pretended to bawl, scrunching my face up.

"Here, this will cheer you up," Matthew offered, as he let the biggest fart blast out his rear end.

"Oh Matthew. That stinks," complained Josh. "You are so revolting. You must be going to be a weather man when you grow up, because you know all about wind and the various types." We all laughed at Josh's joke.

Matthew's reply was another big butt blaster out of his very explosive rear end. Sometimes when Matthew wasn't concentrating, his butt went kamikaze and it started shooting off in all directions. This was one of those times. We all rolled on our backs laughing hysterically. It was so gross, it was funny. Jacob got up and ran away, the smell was so bad. I plugged up my nose until a cool breeze took the ghastly stench upwind.

"Stop it Matthew," I giggled, trying to gain control over my laughing gear so we could talk more about the PS comp. But before I could open my mouth, Elly and Sophie walked over towards us with Nigel in tow; their expressions stony faced. I knew she was going to tell us off for laughing at Matthew's farts. Party pooper! Some girls are such goody goody's.

"SERIOUSLY!" she began. "Are you seriously laughing at a fart like that? That's not a fart! THIS IS A FART!"

And she bent over to the side and let the most overwhelming blaster rip from her butt. It went for about seven seconds. We were speechless, but the sounds of Jacob and Nigel laughing uncontrollably broke the deathly silence. Sophie looked a little embarrassed but she began chuckling as well, quietly at first, but then fiercely as everyone joined in, including me.

That new girl was really hard to work out. After we all collapsed and lay on the ground staring lazily toward the sky, getting our breath back, someone started the game of making objects out of the clouds. I think it was Nigel, but it was really fun. It wasn't until Jacob said he could see a PS controller that it reminded me that it was time to go into the PS club.

"Let's go, Mr H will be unlocking the door to the computer room soon."

"Hey I'm gonna blitz you Rino, if I verse you," Nigel said smugly.

"Yeah whatever you reckon, Nige," I replied, knowing that it *was* a strong possibility. I didn't want to let on that I hadn't been practicing much. I didn't want him being overconfident and praying on my weaknesses.

"Elly and I have been practicing big time. We're gonna smash both of you," he continued.

"I thought you said you didn't have a PS3 Elly," I questioned, seizing the opportunity.

"Oh I didn't, but I had some birthday money left over, so I bought one."

"You bought one? You must have had a lot of money left?"

"No silly. Just a second hand one. There was a yard sale in a house around the corner from me, and this really nice girl gave it to me for a bargain price because I didn't have a lot of money."

"WHAT?" I was dumbfounded.

I was flabbergasted.

I was thunderstruck

"Yes. She said her brother wouldn't mind because he had a PlayStation 4 *and* an XBOX anyway. Then she said he was so dumb, he wouldn't even notice it was gone," she laughed. "She doesn't know how lucky she is to have a brother to do things with though. I wish I had a brother."

"WHAT?" I repeated, little smoke bombs billowing from my head. I was speechless. "H…h…how much did you pay?" I stuttered, not really wanting to hear the answer.

"Ah thirty dollars."

"Thirty dollars?" I cringed. "She put thirty dollars on a two hundred dollar console that had hardly been used?" I wanted to cry. In fact I wanted to scream. I wanted to holler. I wanted to let out a rip roaring, blood curdling screech and tear up the peaceful sky with its fluffy clouds.

"Well not exactly," Elly continued looking at me strangely. "She didn't have a price marked on it. In fact she didn't have it out. I asked if she had any PlayStation 3's for sale, thinking that she wouldn't, but she told me to wait while she went and had a look. I couldn't believe my luck. It was like someone was really looking out

157

for me. Seriously it was the best thing that had ever happened to me in two years, since my mom and dad got divorced."

Why did she have to go and say these things that made me feel sorry for her every time I was about to get mad with her? How was I supposed to know her parents were divorced?

"Wow, for someone who has diabetes and whose parents are divorced, you sure have your sh…. stuff together," Matthew said, nearly letting a swear word pop out.

"Yeah," agreed Josh.

"Yeah," Jacob echoed, because I don't think he really knew what else to say.

"Well you just have to make the best with whatever situation you have I guess. There's heaps worse than me. I feel like I'm pretty lucky actually."

"Really?" Josh queried. "You feel lucky to have divorced parents?"

"No," she laughed. "But, I mean, well it doesn't have to be bad. I feel lucky that I still get to see both my parents. I've come to a new school which is pretty awesome. I've got a really cool teacher, and have met some awesome kids who are cool gamers, and I've met some nice friends." She looked around at Sophie. "*And I* get to play PlayStation at school. Like, WOW. That would never have happened at my old school." She paused. "Ryan, how did you know the console I bought had hardly been used?"

"Huh? Oh, that, ah, I just guessed," I lied.

Matthew nudged me. "Didn't you say that your sister had a yard sa...."

"SSSSSHH." I cut Matthew off before he could say it.

Mr Higginbottom stuck his head out the door just as we approached. "What's got into you gang? You're running late. How are we to have a decent competition if our time is cut short? Don't forget we no longer get the afternoon session in here anymore." He beckoned us in with his hands. "I've got the consoles ready. You just need to pick an enemy."

We looked around at each other, not knowing how we would pick our combatant.

"Don't look so worried my little soldiers," Mr H began. "I have it covered. Ladies first. Elly dive your hand in here and pick out your foe."

"What does foe mean?" asked Matthew.

"Your enemy. Haven't you heard of friend or foe?" Josh was quick to answer. "Come on Mattie, let's get a bean bag and sit down."

"Got the poopcorn?" Matthew said accidentally. "I mean popcorn," he chuckled.

Elly put her hand in and we all stood watching intently, waiting to see who she would verse.

"Ali," she said smiling.

"Doh! I gotta play a girl," he said in a friendly way. That meant I had to verse Nigel, which meant I definitely stood a big chance of losing, which meant......I WAS DOOMED!

159

34. Game on Dudes

"GAME ON BOYS," Mr Higginbottom declared as we took our positions.

"You can't say that, Mr H," I said, looking over at Elly. She smiled in appreciation.

"So……..I'll say…… GAME ON DUDES," he stated.

And we were off.

"Go Rino," cheered Josh.

"Yeah go Rino," echoed Matthew, and then everything except for the game became a blur, as Nigel and I went head to head in the closest ever game I had ever played, like **everrrrrrrrrrrrrrrrr.**

I was the futuristic soldier again because Nigel had been the zombie in the previous game. That suited me and Nigel was more suited to being a zombie anyway if you ask me.

The game was soooooooo close. I built ten buildings. Nigel blasted ten buildings. I spawned eight soldiers. He blasted them all. He blew up heaps of pigions but I got heaps as well.

I couldn't believe it. With thirty seconds to go, Nigel was ten points up, and Mr H began counting down the seconds, which completely took my concentration away, and I couldn't think properly. My mind became a fuzzy haze of zombies shooting at each other.

NOOOOOOOOOO! This could not happen to me. I was the best gamer. I couldn't miss out on the grand final. NO WAY!

35. Don't Throw Money Away

That night, I went home and blasted Lisa for selling my PS3. It ended in a full on screaming match. Actually it pretty well started as a full on screaming match.

"How could you have sold my PS3 without asking me first? I played like a loser because I'd had no practice," I screamed when I walked through the door.

"Sure it wasn't because you *are* a loser?" she sniggered.

"You are such an idiot!" I replied, losing my cool.

"Don't call me an idiot, dork head," she retaliated.

"Don't call me a dork head. You're the dork head for selling my PS3 for what the controller is worth. Don't you know what a PS3 is worth?"

"Not really. Tell someone who cares. Mooooom," she screeched.

"Don't call Mom. Actually, no, call Mom. She needs to hear what you did."

"What's the problem? You said I could sell anything that was in the garage as long as I didn't go anywhere near your bedroom, and as long as I gave you the money for it. So there. I did exactly what you said."

"I never got any money for it!" I exclaimed, getting angrier and angrier.

"Yes you did, I posted it to you through your door, so I didn't have to go in that stinky rodent infested cave you call your bedroom."

My sister is so sweet. NOT! "Grrrrrrrrrrr," I groaned under my breath. How was I possibly going to co-exist in the one house for the rest of my kid years with this......this...... half-witted nincompoop?

"I never got any money!" I repeated.

"It was in a pink envelope with love hearts over the front." I gasped as I vividly remembered seeing a crumpled up pink envelope on the floor, and throwing it into my bin. I raced upstairs shouting to Mom on the way.

"MOM! Have you emptied my bin yet?" Of course she didn't answer me. She has this rule that she won't answer anyone who is not in the same room as her. She has some whacky ideas.

I bounded into my room and upended the bin. Hundreds of items cascaded out, including pencil shavings, old bits of gum, broken army men, a random gold yugioh card that I'd been looking for everywhere, and right at the bottom was the pink envelope. I tore it open, and inside was forty-five dollars in it, and a note from my darling sister which said,

Here is your money from the yard sale. I managed to sell your old PS3 to a nice girl who didn't have one. Love your fav sister Lisa. And she had xx at the end.

I was speechless, again. And I was also pretty happy I had some money to spend. As I went back downstairs, I had to fight with myself to keep pretending I was mad at Lisa, but secretly I was excited to have some cash to spend. And even more secretly, like way down in the pit of my stomach, I was sort of proud of Lisa for being kind to someone that was poorer than us. But I wasn't going to tell her that.

"So how am I supposed to practice for the grand final of the PlayStation 3 competition if I don't have a PlayStation 3? Can you tell me oh favorite sister?"

"Well how was I supposed to know you were in a dumb competition again? And anyway, you have a PlayStation 4. That's better isn't it? Just practice on that." Girls can be so stupid sometimes.

They just don't understand. Well most girls anyway. Elly Gross was the exception.

"Well I don't know. She lives around here somewhere with her dad. Stalk her out and ask to buy it back from her," Lisa suggested. "It's not my fault."

"I don't have to stalk her out. I know exactly where to find her. She's in my grade and I'm going to be versing her in the grand final in two weeks. And every day for two weeks, she's going to be practicing on MY PlayStation."

"So buy it back, or tell someone who cares," and with her unsympathetic words, she left.

"Zit face," I said, under my breath when she had gone.

"I HEARD THAT!" she called out. I started thinking about how I could ask Elly for the PS3 back, but the more I thought about it, the more I realised Lisa was right. I had a PS4 and I also had a proper family, and a sister, even if she was a pain, some of the time anyway; most of the time, actually all of the time.

But as much as I felt sorry for Elly, I decided I would let her keep my PS3, but there was no way I was going to go easy on her in the grand final. I *had* to win. I had to save my reputation as the best gamer in the fifth grade.

So I would have to find a way to practice on the PS3 during the week at Josh or Matthew's house. Instead of playing Minecraft, I would have to talk them into playing Galactic Zombie with me, and I would have to talk Mom into letting me do A LOT of home work at their houses. But a few little white lies would be worth it in the end.

36. Nightmares and Crazy Dreams

The next two weeks were a nightmare. Every day I had to work so hard to make sure I completed all the work and got good marks so I could make the criteria each day. It's hard work being a perfect student I can tell you.

And every night I had to make sure I got my homework done quickly and then race round to Josh or Matthew's house to pretend to do my homework there. I didn't really need to go ballistic practicing, because I knew deep down, Elly was no competition for me. Somehow she'd managed to beat Ali and Sam, but there was no way she stood a chance against me. She was a girl, and most girls couldn't play PlayStation to save their lives.

The night before the big competition, I couldn't get to sleep. I was restless in my bed, tossing and turning, farting and burping; anything that could help pass the time away.

166

I'd double checked with my Mom, like a hundred times, that they weren't going to steal me away in the middle of the night like last time. At the start of the year when Mr H ran the first ever PlayStation comp with a prize, I made it into the grand final, but on the big day, I awoke to find that my family had kidnapped me out of my bed and we were in the car travelling to Movie World for Lisa's birthday. I nearly had a heart attack. It all worked out in the end but for a while it felt like a nuclear bomb had blown up the world.

This time, that was NOT going to happen. I made sure Mom and Dad knew about the competition, and I made sure there were no unpleasant surprises. It was going to be just me versus the zombie at school. No-one was going to get in our way.

Finally after having crazy dreams about Minecraft Endermans and alien zombies going into combat, I drifted off to sleep.

167

I woke up feeling really tired but pumped for the big game. I was so nervous my hand kept spilling the cereal out of the spoon. I was as nervous as a mouse in a room full of mousetraps.

On the way to school, I noticed Nigel walking with Elly. He was probably giving her some tips on how to cheat. I hoped they didn't notice me, so I slowed down so they could get ahead.

But Elly spotted a cat and stopped to pat it, and when she did, she noticed me, even though I was trying to hide behind a bush. I think I probably looked pretty stupid, just hanging around a bush on the way to school.

"Oh hi," Elly said, which made Nigel turn around.

"What are you doing in that bush?" he asked. "Are you some sort of weirdo perv?"

"I'm bird watching," I quickly replied.

"Bird watching?" he said in disbelief. "Bahahaha."

"Yeah Nige, why not? Nothing better to do," I said, as I caught up to them, and tried to pass.

"So are you ready for the big game today?" Elly asked me.

"Yeah 'bout as ready as I'll ever be," I said, trying hard to stay cool.

"I guess you've been practicing a lot?"

"Nope. Don't have a PS3.....anymore."

"Oh, really. You should have said. We could have practiced together," she offered sweetly. But I knew it was fake!

"Seriously! You would practice with the enemy?" She looked at me blankly as if I'd asked her to commit a murder.

"Well, why not? The more practice we have, the better we get, and the more awesome the match we would have. Anyway, it's going to be super fun no matter who wins," and she smiled as she picked up the cat, and began stroking it until it purred.

I didn't know how I was going to make it through the morning, I was so nervous. Algebra, English, spelling, reading, science; boring boring boring!!!

Bring on lunch time!

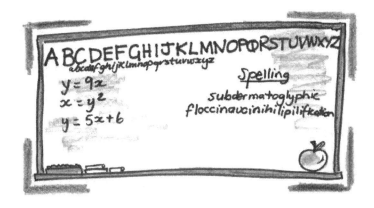

37. Grand Final Number Two

"Ladies and germs, I present to you, Grand Final number two of the greatest PlayStation competition ever in the history of schools. In fact I do believe it is the *only* PlayStation comp in any school, anywhere. For the second grand time in history, LET THE GAMES BEGIN. Good luck fellas." Mr Higginbottom opened our game with a grand speech to half the class that were there to spectate. There were even more kids than when I played Nigel in the first competition at the start of the year. I think it was because this was the first time there was a girl in the competition. Hek this was the first time there was a girl in the whole PS Club.

But unknown to her, she was going down. She was going to get smashed to bits. It wasn't going to be a pretty sight. Zombies trashed into pieces, blasted to bits, is never a pretty sight. I looked over towards the girl. *Sorry Elly*, I thought in my head, *but here goes*.

The speed of the game was incredible. I'd heard Elly was like lightning but I really hadn't believed it. Where had she learned to game like that? Her fingers moved nimbly over the controllers as she pelted me with hail fire as I tried desperately to construct a new city.

With every brick I laid, she blasted the foundations through the solar system. When she wasn't blasting me, she was blowing up the elfions and eating the pigions. Her point score was rising at the speed of lightning.

Finally I was able to grow my team of soldiers and start blasting her zombie, Zed, back, firing the spider gel into its gleaming eyes, and blasting it with radioactive fire. Its lives were stripped away and my point score started to rise rapidly as I made my come back.

My heart started pumping and my breathing rate zoomed as I found myself holding tight until the very last seconds when we were neck and neck in our score. It was 650 points each and Mr Higginbottom began counting down the last thirty seconds, and the crowd of children roared in excitement as I put together the final pieces of an office building. I had 3 more bricks to lay and I would score 100 points, but as I laid the last brick on the building, the zombie swiftly threw a hand grenade at an elfion and Mr Higginbottom yelled "CEASE FIRE" and pressed the stop button. The final scores flashed up with crazy bells alarming.

I didn't know what to think. I didn't know where to look. I was gobsmacked.

I was as flabbergasted as a goldfish sitting on a couch.

I was as shocked as a ghost banging into a wall.

I was as mortified as a superhero realising he can't fly, (after jumping off a skyscraper).

Zed 660 defeated Fire Lasher 650 flashed on the screen.

I was a bigger loser than all the biggest losers put together in the history of the biggest loser.

BEATEN BY A GIRL.

BEATEN BY A GIRL

How was I ever going to face my fans? Not that I had any. But if I did, I definitely wouldn't have any left.

When the game ended, rebel tears threatened to bulge out of my eyes, but I threatened them back. I said I'd punch my eyes out if they escaped, and they didn't like that, so my eyes stayed dry thank goodness.

The rest of the day was an awful blur, full of kids coming up to me and saying bad luck. I wasn't sure whether they were genuine or just making fun of me and joking behind my back. Who knows and who cares right? Well actually, I sort of do.

Of course Elly with the smelly belly became Miss popularity for the day. Everyone wanted to speak to her and congratulate her, tell her how awesome she was, and all I wanted to do was HATE her.

How could she do this to me????

But I couldn't hate her. She *was* awesome. She kicked arse. She kicked arse when we were playing British bulldog and Red Rover, she kicked arse in handball, she kicked arse with her school work, she kicked arse in the final, and worst of all, she kicked my arse when it came down to being just a genuinely friendly person. I hated to say it, but she deserved to win. She was a good kid. I admit it.

On the way home that day, Matthew and Josh were talking about the competition. I kept trying to change the subject and talk about Minecraft. I couldn't wait to get home, chill out for a bit, then jump into the nether, build a city, slam a zombie, do the usual;

anything to take my mind off the final. But they just kept on talking about how cool Galactic Zombie was and how cool Elly was.

"I think I might ask her to the fifth grade disco," Josh announced.

"What?" Matthew and I both said simultaneously as we blurted out laughing. "You're kidding right?" I continued.

"Why not? It's not like I want to ask Furby burbie," Josh replied. That's a nick name we have for Cheryl Burpie.

"You don't have to ask *anyone*. We can just all go together. You don't *have* to have a date," I said, grossing out at the thought. What was Josh thinking?

"Yeah Josh. Don't creep us out man. Save the dates for twelfth grade will ya man. Ooo gross. Now I have this image of Josh and Elly k.i.s.s.i.n.g," said Matthew as he slobbered all over the back of his hand, pretending to kiss it. Josh whacked him gently in mock anger.

"I'm only thinking about it, and anyway, it's a long way off. Can we change the subject?" Josh pleaded, his cheeks blushing slightly. Matthew and I laughed. At least the subject was off the biggest loser; ME. I said my goodbyes and agreed to meet them later on Minecraft.

I mooched down the street feeling sorry for myself. I knew as soon as I got home, Lisa would start stirring me for being a big, fat loser.

Before I got to my street, I saw Elly and Nigel hanging around talking at the corner. They saw me straight away so I couldn't hide or

174

walk the other way. I was sure Nigel would have some slimy comment to make about losing to a girl.

"Hey Ryan," Elly called out as she waved to me. "Awesome game hey."

"Bad luck Rino," Nigel said, as I approached, but this time there was no meanness in his tone. I think he actually meant it. Something had happened to that kid, and I think it had a fair bit to do with the girl that was standing in front of him. "Every time Elly and I practiced, she blitzed me, so you did awesome to come so close," he offered. "Gotta go, I'm running late. Catch yas," and he took off quickly, leaving Elly and I standing alone awkwardly. At least, *I* was feeling awkward.

OMG was all I could think. I'd never been alone with a girl before. What was I supposed to say to her? But Elly was so easy going, she knew exactly what to say.

"It was so cool playing against you today. You are the most awesome player I've ever versed, and I've played some pretty tough gamers back home." I blushed, secretly beaming inside.

"Really? How did you get to play tough guys, you know, being a girl and all?"

"I belonged to a PS club, out of school though. I was the only girl."

"Girls were allowed in the club?" I asked, in astonishment.

"Of course silly. This is the twenty first century. What club would dare to be so sexist and not allow girls?"

"Yeah right, of course, how dumb of me," I said, feeling very foolish. "No wonder you're so good at it." She laughed as we walked casually along. "So what game are you going to get with the prize?"

"Ah, I've already done something with it," she said.

"Yeah? That was quick. What did you get?" Elly seemed reluctant to answer. "So….. you got …..?" I prompted.

"I gave the voucher to Nigel."

"WHAT?" I said, astounded. "He didn't bully you for it did he?" I said, suddenly feeling protective over the girl. Elly laughed at me again.

"Of course not. He would never do that."

"Yeah right. Are we talking about the same kid?"

"Oh he's harmless. You've just got to know how to treat him. He wants attention and to feel important. He's going through some hard times with his family. I gave Nigel the voucher as a thank you, because when I first came to this school, he really helped me. He gave me time and help when nobody else did. I just wanted to repay him somehow."

"WOW! That's really cool of you."

"It's nothing," she replied, as we approached a small rundown cottage. "Well this is my house. It looks a bit messy because Dad's renovating it."

"Ok see ya. Well done for today, even if you did beat me," I said, not knowing what else to say.

"Ryan," she began, but then hesitated, "Oh nothing," and she ran up the cobbled pathway before turning around and calling out to me again. "Don't suppose you want to go to the fifth grade disco with me?"

I hoped she didn't hear the gulp that got stuck in my throat as I babbled out my words. "Sure," I dribbled out, wondering what Josh would say.

I think I just got myself into my first teenage sticky situation. And I'm not even a teenager.

If only girls weren't allowed at the disco, life would be so much easier.

THE END

Don't forget, if you liked this book, please tell your friends and leave a review on Amazon or Goodreads. Then I'll know to keep writing more adventures about the PS club.

gameonboysseries@gmail.com

Made in the USA
Middletown, DE
16 January 2016

walk the other way. I was sure Nigel would have some slimy comment to make about losing to a girl.

"Hey Ryan," Elly called out as she waved to me. "Awesome game hey."

"Bad luck Rino," Nigel said, as I approached, but this time there was no meanness in his tone. I think he actually meant it. Something had happened to that kid, and I think it had a fair bit to do with the girl that was standing in front of him. "Every time Elly and I practiced, she blitzed me, so you did awesome to come so close," he offered. "Gotta go, I'm running late. Catch yas," and he took off quickly, leaving Elly and I standing alone awkwardly. At least, *I* was feeling awkward.

OMG was all I could think. I'd never been alone with a girl before. What was I supposed to say to her? But Elly was so easy going, she knew exactly what to say.

"It was so cool playing against you today. You are the most awesome player I've ever versed, and I've played some pretty tough gamers back home." I blushed, secretly beaming inside.

"Really? How did you get to play tough guys, you know, being a girl and all?"

"I belonged to a PS club, out of school though. I was the only girl."

"Girls were allowed in the club?" I asked, in astonishment.

"Of course silly. This is the twenty first century. What club would dare to be so sexist and not allow girls?"

"Yeah right, of course, how dumb of me," I said, feeling very foolish. "No wonder you're so good at it." She laughed as we walked casually along. "So what game are you going to get with the prize?"

"Ah, I've already done something with it," she said.

"Yeah? That was quick. What did you get?" Elly seemed reluctant to answer. "So….. you got …..?" I prompted.

"I gave the voucher to Nigel."

"WHAT?" I said, astounded. "He didn't bully you for it did he?" I said, suddenly feeling protective over the girl. Elly laughed at me again.

"Of course not. He would never do that."

"Yeah right. Are we talking about the same kid?"

"Oh he's harmless. You've just got to know how to treat him. He wants attention and to feel important. He's going through some hard times with his family. I gave Nigel the voucher as a thank you, because when I first came to this school, he really helped me. He gave me time and help when nobody else did. I just wanted to repay him somehow."

"WOW! That's really cool of you."

"It's nothing," she replied, as we approached a small rundown cottage. "Well this is my house. It looks a bit messy because Dad's renovating it."

"Ok see ya. Well done for today, even if you did beat me," I said, not knowing what else to say.

"Ryan," she began, but then hesitated, "Oh nothing," and she ran up the cobbled pathway before turning around and calling out to